A BALLET-MAKER's
HANDBOOK

A BALLET-MAKER'S HANDBOOK

Sources · Vocabulary · Styles

Joan Lawson

A & C Black · London
Theatre Arts Books/Routledge · New York

First published 1991
by A & C Black (Publishers) Limited
35 Bedford Row, London WC1R 4JH

ISBN 0-7136-3246-1

Published simultaneously in USA
by Theatre Arts Books
in association with Routledge, Chapman & Hall, Inc.
29 West 35th Street, New York, NY 10001

ISBN 0-87830-017-1

© 1991 Joan Lawson

CIP catalogue records for this book
are available from the British Library
and from the Library of Congress.

Printed in Great Britain
by Whitstable Litho Ltd,
Whitstable, Kent

This book is dedicated to the memory of

Sir Frederick Ashton CH, OM

whose long friendship, wise and sympathetic counsel
and enthusiasm for the art of dance made it possible.

'I am a happy man to have brought off what I
set out to do and happy at the public's response.
Yours, Freddie'

In a note to the author after the first night of *Symphonic Variations*

Contents

Illustrations/acknowledgements
arranged alphabetically by ballet

Preface

When the late P.J.S. Richardson invited me to become critic of *The Dancing Times* (1940) he asked me to concentrate on the choreography of the ballets reviewed. He knew it would be possible as I had done some historical study and had been introduced to dance as a child, when he first knew me, by Margaret Morris. She was the first to realise that, to succeed in modern dance, one needed a firm basis of technique, a vocabulary of steps and poses and a grammar or what she called 'choregraphy'. At her dancing lessons there were sometimes choreographic problems to solve: perhaps a list of steps to weave in a pattern on the floor or in the air; or a short story, one line of a poem or an idea to express in dance; or, better still, to improvise from or interpret a piece of music in a more set form in order to display its rhythm, theme or aspects of its construction. In 1940 I was also trying to use Margaret Morris' choreographic teaching to create a few dances for myself. I was lecturing on dance and ballet for the Central Advisory Council for Education among HM Forces and needed appropriate illustrations for the topics discussed and demonstrated.

Until 1940 most ballet criticism in England was written by leading music critics, to whom the task had been given on the arrival of Diaghilev because most of his scores had been specially commissioned and needed expert analysis. It is to some of those critics that I owe my deepest gratitude. They were masters in many fields and their patience and help in answering my questions encouraged me throughout my years as critic. Edwin Evans was an authority on French music, a musical adviser to Diaghilev and later to Ninette de Valois; Frank Howes was chief music critic of *The Times* – his knowledge of folk music and dance and of music hall comedians fitted easily into his other capacity as musicologist; Philip Hope Wallace, that tower of musical learning whose talk could range from primitive and ancient music to the most contemporary, from oratorio to opera, from operetta to musical comedy and popular songs, from ballads to jazz and the latest craze from Tin Pan Alley. Finally there was Scott Goddard whose extra speciality was Indian dance and music. I also had valuable help from the Soviet critics and historians Natalie Rosslavleva, Yuri Ossipovitch Slonimsky and Yuri Alexeevitch Bakroushine, who befriended me when I first visited the USSR in 1938.

My introduction to the work of the great Russian choreographers was in the classroom of Seraphina Astafieva and, later, in conversation with other Diaghilev dancers such as Tamara Karsavina, Serge Grigoriev, Lubov Tchernicheva and Lydia Sokolova. Finally I studied with Fokine himself through long talks with him and Edwin Evans, usually at the piano – perhaps my most precious memories.

The first task my mentors set me when I started out as critic was to define style in ballet. They argued that once a choreographer had been inspired to create a work based on some story, theme or music, a decision had to be made about the style of dance that would be the most appropriate form of expression. They were undoubtedly urged to ask this question after noting the range of styles adopted by choreographers such as Perrot, Petipa, Fokine, Massine and Balanchine of the Diaghilev era. This range was further developed through the work of Frederick Ashton, Ninette de Valois and others.

After much discussion my mentors finally agreed that the range of styles used by choreographers could be roughly divided into five categories: classical, *demi-caractère*, romantic, character and/or national, and modern.

Perhaps it is understandable that we could never quite agree as to what was meant by 'modern' ballet. The *Oxford English Dictionary* was not much help although its definition of Modernism

> To subordinate tradition to harmonise with modern thought or modern terms of expression

admirably described Nijinska's *Les Noces* (1923).

Until his death some twenty years later, Edwin Evans continued to insist that *Les Noces* was the most modern of classical ballets because, although its roots lay in ancient marriage rites, the form was seen and heard through the eyes and ears of a contemporary choreographer, composer and artist, and performed by their contemporaries. The dancers used their bodies as ancient peoples had done in order to make their movement expressive but their minds were modern. *Les Noces* in 1923 was contemporary also because it reflected the general trends and theories expounded by the painters, sculptors, writers and musicians of the period.

Since then, many theories about the causes and significance of all kinds of movement have been put forward by psychologists, psychotherapists, scientists, dancers and others dissatisfied with what they term the artificialities of classical ballet. Yet for all such efforts the human body remains the same expressive medium upon which all choreographers work. Fokine broke down many of the conventional artificialities with his first works as choreographer in 1904. Others have followed his example. Today it is far more difficult to define exactly to which category a ballet does belong than it was in the nineteenth and early twentieth centuries.

Fortunately, some choreographers, and they are major ones, still conform to the earlier definitions. I have, therefore, used their works as the basis for this book and print the definitions my mentors and I agreed upon as an introduction to each section on style.

Les Noces   The first modern ballet – Nijinska's interpretation of contemporary aesthetics
Above: the Bridesmaids; below: the Bridegroom's friends (The Royal Ballet)

INTRODUCTION

Ballet-making: a brief analysis

Choreography is the art of design through dance. It is created by a choreographer who wishes to communicate some story, theme or musical expression to an audience. He hopes that through his combination of dance steps, poses and gestures the onlookers will understand and feel the meaning of his work.

Choreographic design is not the whole ingredient of a ballet. Ballet has always been a theatre art in which other artists are involved. Their contribution to the whole has varied in importance but it is only within recent years that certain choreographers have decided to do without one or another or all the other arts. Such experimental works cannot be called ballets in the traditional sense of the word. From earliest days, ballets have been likened to a poem, a comic or tragic tale, or as 'living music' (the late Ernest Newman). They relate to any one of these other arts because they have drawn inspiration and colour from them. Those ballets that have stood the test of time have been created by choreographers in collaboration not only with authors, librettists and composers but also with stage designers and technicians, all of whom set out to provide the many faceted setting within which the dancers move.

Ballet is an art of generalisations that reflects particular events through dance. It can hold a mirror up to life as other arts do, but the vehicle for expression is dance on the stage. Performers have to convince their audience of reality by conveying, without saying a word, the moods, emotions and behaviour of the characters played. The portraying of life through dance is not new. Primitive tribes everywhere have enacted through dance all the activities which form part of life. It is from such ancient sources that the techniques of both Western and Eastern classical dance have developed and inspired many ballets. Performances still occur somewhere in the world. They record or celebrate a range of activities from a successful hunting expedition, the sowing and reaping of corn, a fight and resultant victory over the enemy, prayers for rain and the sun or moon, to celebrating a wedding. Other dances relate to the birth and death of the year.

These were the origin of certain Greek and Roman myths and legends which later underlay the death and resurrection rites of the early Christian Church and which were transformed during the Renaissance into such fairy tales as *The Sleeping Beauty* (France) and *The Firebird* (Russia). Greek and Roman tales of great heroes, such as the works of Homer and Virgil, and other European and Asian epics have inspired ballets which depict the struggle between good and evil, love and hate, life and death, and, during the Romantic era, the struggle between the world of the flesh and the world of the spirit (the source of such ballets as *Giselle* and *La Sylphide*).

The work of the ballet-maker or choreographer

Ballet-makers are designers of expressive dance. In common with all other artists they are inspired to convey ideas, thoughts and impressions to an audience. However they are different from most other artists in that they work directly on living material. The active process of design begins when they first meet the dancers who are to communicate the idea. Thus they have to mould and shape the dancers' movements and to stir their imagination in such a way that they can convey the purpose of the design across the footlights.

The subjects choreographers choose to depict on stage can range from a simple design in dance movement to the most complex of stories. Whatever they wish to communicate they must first make the meaning clear to the dancers. Balletmasters should, therefore, be able to match the dance design and the music by studying the rhythm, phrasing, form, time signature, tempo and other details of composition. If need be they must create gestures which will enable the dancers to convey the moods, emotions and actions of the story or theme. The choreographer should explain to the dancers their status, behaviour, habits, work or pastimes. The dance movements should be suitable for the environment in which they live for the duration of the stage time allowed. The dance design should be formed in such a way that it has its own style and expression, reinforced by the rhythm and style of the music, the appropriate scenery and costumes, and the location and atmosphere of the whole design.

Whatever choreographers wish to communicate by way of story, theme or musical interpretation, they must possess a large vocabulary of dance steps, poses and gestures upon which to build their design, no matter in which style they compose their movements. And this is not enough. They must understand the effect that moods, emotions and actions have on the human body so that they can make dancers feel the effects for themselves if they are to convince the audience of the truth of their dance.

Today's choreographers need a thorough knowledge of the vocabulary of classical ballet and of the generally accepted forms of character dance upon which most nineteenth and early twentieth century ballets were based. They should have some knowledge of anatomy and of at least one system of modern dance. Mere acquaintance only with the three types of mime is inadequate. Long before he died, Fokine had already buried these stereotyped forms in a broader form of expression which he called mimed dance or danced mime, thereby freeing his dancers from the ancient conventions of Court and Imperial ballets, which Petipa had so firmly preserved. A broad and appreciative knowledge of the other arts must be the final recommendation.

PART 1
SOURCES OF INSPIRATION

In this book the work of the choreographers obviously takes pride of place but the examples illustrating the text all needed composers for the score, artists for the sets and costumes, experts in lighting, technicians of all kinds and above all dancers to interpret the choreographic design. Moreover, choreographers cannot work without some source of inspiration. Where are today's aspirants to find a source if they have no ideas of their own and if one has not been suggested to them?

It is not always appreciated that many successful ballets have been suggested by people on the fringe of the ballet world. One of the best examples of this kind of help were the ideas given by Gautier, the French poet and journalist, to Saint-Georges the librettist. Gautier so admired the dancing of Carlotta Grisi that he suggested two themes which produced *Giselle*. The director of the Bolshoi Theatre felt he would have a financial success on his hands if he could persuade Tchaikovsky to write a score. When the composer expressed willingness and said that he would like a story from the age of chivalry, the director with the help of a German balletmaster worked out the plot of *Swan Lake*. Khudekov, editor of a St. Petersburg newspaper, suggested that Petipa should create ballets based on the news of the day and provided several librettos. One of the most successful was *The Daughter of Pharaoh* staged when the excavations in Egypt were a favourite topic of conversation. The artist Benois was responsible for the librettos of *Le Pavillon d'Armide* and *Petrushka*. The latter is still one of the finest examples of a collaboration between three masters of their own art: Benois, Stravinsky and Fokine. But would their work have been so successful without Diaghilev, that genius whose gift for matching artist to artist in the service of his dancers was and still is unique in history.

Dance

It is not easy for today's audiences and choreographers to understand that in the earliest days of ballet, balletmasters were very little concerned with dance except as a social accomplishment. Their task was to 'teach the delicate art of court dance' together with correct behaviour and rules of precedence. When the learned writers such as the Pléiade and, later, members of the Académie Royale had decided on the purpose and meaning of the spectacle to be staged, it was the balletmasters who ensured that the dancers' movements conformed to the perfect steps and patterns. These might or might not have significance for the onlookers. From that time (1564) until the early twentieth century, with some rare exceptions, ballets were still being produced roughly on the same lines. The spectacle was more important than the development of plot and character.

It was not until Bournonville's *Konservatoriet* (1849) that dance itself became the subject of a ballet. It was staged because Bournonville wished to impress upon Copenhagen the importance of his work as balletmaster. One scene of this ballet is still performed. It finds his pupils of all ages and competence at work in the classroom using many of his exercises. This idea was later to inspire other choreographers, among them Ashton who brought to life Degas' wonderful sketches of *les petits rats* of the Paris Opera (*Foyer de Danse*) and Harold Lander (*Etudes*).

In 1901 social dance away from the classroom inspired Gorsky, the Moscow balletmaster, to create the first of the so-called abstract ballets. Since then choreographers have often explored dance in a social context and in the same kind of setting as the early balletmasters, creating the incidents that can occur during a dance or ballet. This theme has enormous scope if one considers only a handful of ballets. There are the charming lovers' meetings and partings of Ashton's *Les Rendezvous* and an alternative treatment in Robbins' *Dances at a Gathering*. The latter has some lovely moments when the young people pause to wonder at the beauty of the day, their happiness and friendship. Neither ballet is like Robbins' hilarious *Fancy Free* where three sailors on shore leave meet three girls in a New York bar, nor like Nijinska's *Les Biches* with the sophisticated behaviour of guests at a house party. This again is in absolute contrast to the hearty goings-on of De Mille's *Rodeo* with its cowboys and girls. In Lichine's *Graduation Ball* teenage cadets meet schoolgirls and cut their

Elite Syncopations   MacMillan's view of 'pop' culture 'Go for it' (The Royal Ballet)

capers. In addition there is the extraordinary behaviour of some of the clientele in the low dive of MacMillan's *Elite Syncopations*.

All the above ballets, despite their variety, can be danced only by classically trained dancers. This is because each requires an acute sense of timing if the many subtleties are to make some impact and to arouse the audience's appreciation and laughter. There are jokes ranging from the most delicate to broad humour that includes old-fashioned slapstick. In some cases deliberately clumsy mishandling requires the greatest dexterity from those involved if the joke is to come off (see also Part 2).

Music

Contrary to general belief music had never been a source of inspiration to choreographers until 1901. Previously, every score had been ordered by a balletmaster, who would hand the composer a list of what was required. Petipa's libretto for *The Sleeping Beauty* gave Tchaikovsky all the choreographic details he needed to know, whether for the *scènes* or *pas d'action*, *variations* or *divertissements*. Among the details were the number of bars, time-signature, tempo, what they represented and sometimes even the instruments Petipa preferred.

Petipa was merely following in a long line of balletmasters who, from the earliest days to the beginning of the eighteenth century, were also the composers, musicians and teachers. Their rules were law and they dominated the production. In 1901, Gorsky created the first abstract ballet to Glinka's *Valse Fantaisie*. He was inspired to parallel in dance the melodic phrasings, rhythms and development of the themes in the score.

Gorsky's example of the interpretation of music was followed by Fokine who used Chopin's music for *Les Sylphides*, Saint-Saëns' for *The Dying Swan* (his unforgettable masterpiece for Anna Pavlova), Schumann's music for *Le Carnaval* and Weber's *Invitation to the Waltz* for *Spectre de la Rose* for Nijinsky.

It was only when Fokine and Stravinsky joined forces to create *The Firebird* and *Petrushka* that an equal partnership between dance and music was formed. It was this relationship which proved to be one of the most important legacies left to the ballet world by Diaghilev and his Ballets Russes.

Since the death of Diaghilev, and particularly since 1945, choreographers have increasingly been inspired by music of both major and minor composers and have created ballets which can be straightforward interpretations of the score as they hear and feel it as, for example, Massine's *Choreartium* (Brahms Fourth Symphony), Balanchine's ballet based on Bach's Double Violin Concerto and *Ballet Imperial* (Tchaikovsky's Second Piano Concerto) and Ashton's five abstract ballets (see p.42).

The list of ballets interpreting music has grown enormously. In the case of those mentioned above the choreographers have found ways to parallel their dance with the rhythms, phrasings and structure of the score. Many have also attempted to catch the overall atmosphere, mood and emotional content. Success requires that choreographers have some knowledge of music as an art in its own right. If not, they should seek advice from experts of the calibre of the late Edwin Evans and Constant Lambert who did so much to further the careers of both choreographers and dancers in the early days of what is now the Royal Ballet.

Literature

Literature from all over the world has always been a source of inspiration. It includes the most ancient myths and legends and the fairy tales which grew from them, the Bible, drama, novels which have given rise to operas then ballets, poetry, even biographies and philosophical essays. A choreographer may be inspired to tell a truly epic tale within three acts and several scenes. Or he may take a brief statement from a full-length play or poem and within twenty minutes depict the whole import. This is what Helpmann did with *Hamlet*. He was inspired by the line from Shakespeare's play: For in that sleep of death what dreams may come – an old belief that at the moment of death all the incidents of a lifetime flash through the memory.

In *The Dream* Ashton depicted only the incidents that took place in the Athenian wood and produced one of the most enchanting Shakespearean ballets. Yet despite its brevity it includes all the ingredients of the great playwright's work. There is something for everybody: lyric poetry, drama and both subtle and broad comedy. It could be called a literal interpretation of the play.

Gloria MacMillan's modern classicism and interpretation of words
Left: 'the fate that held our youth within its power';

'Waited its hour' – the last survivor (Wayne Eagling and The Royal Ballet)

MacMillan, however, made a more profound statement when he took a brief passage from Vera Brittain's *Testament of Youth* to inspire his interpretation of Poulenc's *Gloria*:

Their dreams of happiness
We thought secure
while imminent and fierce outside the door
watching a generation grow to flavour
The fate that held our youth within its power
Waited its hour.

He interpreted the words so poignantly and sincerely that those sensitive to the tragedy of war, the lost hopes of youth who would never know the joy of life and love, felt the true impact of the ballet. Moreover, the irony of setting this choreographic poem to Poulenc's *Gloria* and the stark reality of Klundecis' costumes strengthened the impression made by the choreography.

The above examples demonstrate how it is possible for a choreographer to interpret his source as a literal translation of a story or theme, or as the disclosure of an inner meaning. This had happened already in the first *ballets de cour*. Scholars supplied in every detail the allegory and symbolism demanded by the kings and prelates at whose courts the entertainments were staged. The balletmasters produced the ballets by devising suitable dance patterns.

Myths and legends

A fruitful source for plots has always been the Greek and Roman myths and legends and the epic poems of Eastern and Western peoples which deal with great heroes and heroines. Whether the characters are mortal or immortal, their behaviour is much the same. In other words, they are generalisations.

However some choreographers prefer to tell these old tales in the simplest terms. One of the finest examples is Balanchine's *Apollo* (1929) to Stravinsky's music. Despite the antiquity of the myth it remains one of the most modern ballets in the classical style. Balanchine preserved its balanced, calm and spacious form but extended the movements by doing away with all the constricting conventions his dancers used in the classroom. His three Muses of Dance, Music and Poetry expressed the qualities of their art as they taught the young god. Each gesture had a particular meaning within the flowing movement and because these had always been in the vocabulary of stage gesture the audience understands. Like Fokine before him, Balanchine realised the value of making them part of the total dance, although they are not so softly rounded as in the former's *Les Sylphides*. This difference in style is dictated by the more strongly rhythmic and far less lyrical quality of Stravinsky's music, which in no way resembled the romantic atmosphere of Chopin's score.

Apollo Balanchine's modern classicism
Apollo and the Muses (Wayne Eagling, Fiona Chadwick, Bryony Brind, Deidre Eyden)

Many choreographers have translated old myths and legends in the same simple way as Balanchine because they recognise that the subjects are universally known. In the same way, choreographers have adopted fairy tales that developed from myths at the time of the Renaissance when scholars tried to reconcile the pagan and Christian beliefs. This knowledge became part of the inheritance of dancing masters working in European, Imperial and State Theatres. Even Petipa was aware that the tale of *The Sleeping Beauty*, first told by Perrault in 1635, descended from old death and resurrection rites. Petipa was also acquainted with other traditions such as the language of flowers and their symbolism, and the teaching of the French dance academicians with their insistence on a particular relationship between step and music. But Petipa was wise enough to allow such knowledge to be hidden in his choreography. He did not require his audiences to have erudite knowledge. The classical technique of dance was his most powerful medium with passages of conventional mime to tell the story. Many other choreographers followed his example until Fokine showed how it was possible to eliminate the static passages by using what he called danced mime or mimed dance (see page 58).

The allegorical potential of myths and legends was invaluable to those producing court and opera ballets in which words were all important. The ballets were produced mainly for political purposes and had of necessity to convey some message. They were the result of great efforts 'To hide truth in myth and image'. For example, the *Balet Comique de lo Royne* (1581), one of the first of these, was devised for the wedding of the Catholic Duc de Joyeuse and the Protestant Marguerite de Lorraine when it was hoped that the marriage would unite the warring factions so that 'All would be well in the fair land of France'. The libretto was based on the story of Jason and the Argonauts and their stay in Circe's garden. The scholars wove allegory and symbolism into the words spoken and sung, the music, the designs of the scenery, props and costumes as well as the pattern of the dances.

This type of allegorical ballet continued and is still produced by such choreographers as Martha Graham who seek to disclose the inner meaning of such fables. Kurt Jooss' *The Green Table* (1932) is a modern example of the type of ballet performed in sixteenth-century courts. It was staged as a protest at the signing of the Peace Treaty of Versailles and the rise of Nazism. MacMillan's *Gloria* is another outstanding example of protest. It drew this remark from a fifteen-year-old boy: 'Now I know why there must be no more war.'

Some modern ballets are the result of a choreographer's study of research carried out by Freud and his fellow psychologists and psychotherapists into complex mental processes and problems or, as they were discussed once on a BBC Radio 4 programme, 'The background of the mind'. When created by Martha Graham and MacMillan, these ballets can be very successful – for example, *The Invitation* and *My Brothers, My Sisters* – but it is a difficult task for the choreographer. This is because audiences unacquainted with such theories, even when they have been widely publicised in the press, fail to understand the meaning. As Fokine said: 'If a ballet has to be explained in words, it is not a proper ballet. Never read the libretto on a programme. The dancers say what has to be said.'

Young choreographers should remember that today's audience for ballet is no longer an exclusive clientele of courtiers whose education ensured they fully understood the implications of particular allegory and symbolism. Today the audience is drawn from many cultures, classes and tastes.

The Bible

The most outstanding examples of biblical inspiration are Balanchine's *The Prodigal Son* (1929), de Valois' *Job* (1931) and Ashton's *The Wise Virgins* (1940). Despite their common source they were very different in style, music and décor. Their differences were due first to the collaboration with the composers and designers of each work and secondly to the paintings which inspired all three choreographers.

The Balanchine, Prokofiev, Rouault *The Prodigal Son* was contemporary in every way, each artist being involved in the aesthetic movements of the day. Balanchine's angular, athletic dance, despite his use of *pointes* for the Siren, reflected Prokofiev's dissonant, sparse but strongly rhythmic score. It also reflected the strong elementary colours and outline of Rouault's simple design. All three artists were profoundly interested by and had been involved in religious ceremonial at some time.

De Valois used her own style of plastique for *Job*. This was a flowing expansive style of dance derived from the principles of classical technique but concentrating on the lines of movement necessary to form and re-form tableaux inspired by Blake's illustrations for *The Book of Job*. This work required very careful study because of Blake's superb feeling for movement within the framework and dimension of each picture. De Valois captured this feeling. The audience could turn the pages of Blake's *The Book of Job* whilst watching how the dancers flowed from one picture to form another within the confines of the set and the simple melodies, rhythms and ritual sounds of Vaughan Williams' music. He called *Job* 'a Masque for Dancing', basing each item on the tempo, form and quality of songs and dances used in Elizabethan Masques and Church services.

Ashton's *The Wise Virgins* (lost in the Netherlands when that country was invaded in 1941) was inspired by Renaissance paintings from which Rex Whistler drew inspiration for his exquisite set and costumes. It was danced to music by Bach arranged by Constant Lambert. Despite the seemingly rich setting, Ashton's choreography was simplicity itself and marked by the beautifully phrased *ports de bras* for the Chosen Bride. Into them Ashton wove gestures seen in many Renaissance paintings of the Virgin, saints and angels. These were the same gestures used by monks and nuns during their hours of silence and described in a tenth-century document. Ashton phrased them into purely classical forms to interpret a score which precluded any excess of movement or extravagant posturing.

There have been other works based on biblical themes, none of which has remained famous despite apparent importance at the time of production. A notable example was *David* (1935), specially created for Anton Dolin by Keith Lester to music by Jacobsen, with a magnificent act drop by Epstein and décor by Bernard Meninsky.

Drama

Greek plays based on myth and legend and later dramas have proved to be valuable sources of inspiration. The plays of Shakespeare have especially attracted choreographers, the earliest version of *Romeo and Juliet* being produced in St. Petersburg in 1809.

Twelfth Night, The Taming of the Shrew, The Merry Wives of Windsor, Othello and *Antony and Cleopatra* have all been translated into ballet mostly in the USSR. Several choreographers have used Tchaikovsky's Fantasy Overture, *Romeo and Juliet*, for *pas*

The Prodigal Son   Balanchine's modern classicism
Above: the Son and his Friends on their way to the Inn; below: the Siren (Rudolf Nureyev, Vivian
Lorrayne and The Royal Ballet)

de deux and Nureyev used the same composer's Symphonic Fantasia, *The Tempest*, when he sought to interpret that Shakespearean masterpiece. Tchaikovsky himself admitted he was only composing an impression of that great play: 'The sea, storm, the magic of an island, young love and a wise magician.' He did not attempt any interpretation of individual episodes as he did in *Hamlet* and other tone poems such as *Francesca da Rimini*.* Nureyev's ballet did not mirror Shakespeare's words: 'We are such stuff as dreams are made of', perhaps because reliance was placed on technical devices and lighting rather than on the dancers' involvement in the plot.

Few such ballets have been made in England because the actors' ways of spinning and acting out the words of England's greatest dramatist have inhibited such ideas. To translate those words into movement is difficult because the words range so rapidly from the lyrical, rhetorical, descriptive and humorous to the vulgar and bawdy. They are used in repartee, in passion and in the struggle between good and evil. Fantasy as well as reality can be found in words which express mood, emotion and action. Words are given power and meaning by the varying tones of the actors' voices and the expressiveness of their gestures. Other nationalities can attempt these masterpieces in their own language, but it is in the end the actor steeped in English language and culture – and probably native-born – who excels in Shakespeare's tragedy or comedy.

English choreographers face a particular problem when translating Shakespeare plays into ballet. Those so far chosen for treatment are already known to large numbers of their audience. Any deviation from the text raises eyebrows and even resentment when some important situation arises which signals one of the famous speeches and nothing directly replaces it in the resultant ballet.

Yet balletic interpretations of Shakespeare have proved possible. *Romeo and Juliet* as choreographed by Lavrovsky for the Kirov (1940), Ashton for the Royal Danish Ballet (1955) and MacMillan for the Royal Ballet (1960) have all been successful. The reason would seem to be that all three versions were firmly based on the same music that had originally been commissioned from Prokofiev in the 1930s for an earlier ballet on the subject. Prokofiev composed his music with the help of a famous Soviet theatre director and expert on Shakespeare who insisted that Shakespeare's development and continuity of plot remained intact. He eliminated only those brief scenes and descriptive passages not immediately pertinent to the tragedy of the two lovers and where the confrontations between the quarrelling Montagues and Capulets became too intrusive. Prokofiev seized upon this division of forces by creating what can be called two distinct musical idioms to give each scene its appropriate atmosphere. Firstly there are lyrical passages to herald the joys of youth, the early dances of Juliet and her friends which develop into her awakening love of Romeo and then to the passionate soaring sounds as the lovers embrace in the Balcony and Bedroom scenes only to die sadly away as death comes to both. The second idiom creates the heavy doom-laden atmosphere of the street scenes which increase in intensity as the thunderous clashing of swords between Montague and Capulet leads to death, when the enormity of the quarrel reaches its climax as Lady Capulet mourns over Tybalt's body.

Like the quarrelling families the two Prokofiev idioms are always quarrelling with each other, first one then the other gaining supremacy as the performers stretch themselves to respond to those insistent sounds and the choreographer's wish to express the content of Shakespeare's words to their fullest.

*This was the basis for Lichine's ballet of 1937.

MacMillan's version of *Romeo and Juliet* was intended from the beginning as a three-act ballet. It aimed to interpret the main action as set down by Shakespeare. However the words which described the characters, moods and emotions were replaced by expressive dance woven into long phrases. Those created by MacMillan are particularly interesting to study and not only because they intimately follow the lead given by Prokofiev's music.

Their outstanding features are found in the steps and poses woven into Juliet's leitmotifs (see page 61). First seen when she shyly dances with Paris on being introduced to her kinsman, they are the movements of a child. They seem as if she is taking her first lesson in social contact. They are then repeated when she begins to dance with Romeo at the ball. But as her confidence and feelings grow, so do the movements until she is lifted joyously into the air held by his strong arms before falling into his embrace. These joyous phrases take on greater lightness and passion in the Balcony and then the Bedroom scenes where they acquire poignancy and fear at losing the beloved. What is so important to the development of the action is the way MacMillan uses the same leitmotifs to describe Juliet's relationship with Paris. When she dances with him at the ball, she does not give herself into his hands as she gradually does to Romeo, she keeps her distance; and when he comes to her in the bedroom and tries to repeat his first attempts to woo her, she withdraws herself to the utmost limits, keeping her head averted as she tries to get away before finally falling to the ground.

Similar leitmotifs are used to describe how Romeo develops from the fun-loving man about town, who jokes with his friends and dances with the ladies of the street, to the ardent lover who yet fights fiercely for the honour of his dead friend. The choreographic development of the ballet owes its success to MacMillan's understanding of Prokofiev's score. With its help he has translated Shakespeare's words into dance which can only be performed by those who feel and act the tragedy and know how to convey its meaning.

There was no such specially commissioned score for *Hamlet* (1942). Helpmann used Tchaikovsky's Fantasy Overture, a tone poem inspired by Shakespeare's play. In it the composer attempted to illustrate the words of the play which Helpmann took as his text (see page 20). In the brief space of some twenty minutes the whole of Hamlet's tragedy was seen to flash past. He created few dances but such was his understanding that in the timing of gesture and the theatrical effects of Hamlet's confrontation with first one then another protagonist he caught the moods, emotions and action of the drama. No wonder the critic Edwin Evans said: 'You caught your breath as the curtain rose – held it – and as the curtain fell – sighed with relief.' The production was a triumph for the English dancers involved. For too long they had been dismissed lightly as efficient dancers who lacked expression. Helpmann proved that with the right vehicle they could act as convincingly as they moved, and make their audiences believe in the truth of their play.

To compare Helpmann's highly dramatic *Hamlet* and its swift résumé of Shakespeare's play with Ashton's lyrical and delicately funny *The Dream* may seem ridiculous. Yet in construction they are very similar. In both, the music was specially chosen. (Music for *The [Midsummer Night's] Dream* was arranged by John Lanchbery from Mendelssohn's incidental music to the play.) In both, some characters with their speeches and situations were eliminated. What was left was translated into expressive movement. That Helpmann and Ashton could reduce long plays of varying moods, emotions and actions into brief one-act ballets and still make sense of the core of the plot reinforces even more strongly the remark made by that great English comedian, George Robey: 'The eye is quicker to seize on the meaning of a gesture than the ear to understand the meaning of the words.' Young choreographers should remember it. But there the similarity ends for Ashton worked almost entirely in the world of fantasy, even when that world was penetrated by the mortal lovers and Mechanicals, for Bottom's predicament when straying into the 'magicked Athenian woods' was engineered by the mischievous sprite Puck (see page 125) with his 'herb moly'.

It may also seem ridiculous to compare Ashton's *The Dream* with *A Month in the Country*. Yet their construction is similar. First because they rely on specially chosen music. Secondly, in both, as in *Hamlet*, certain characters and situations have been eliminated and the rest translated into expressive dance. This elimination of long passages, by which Shakespeare and Turgenev had given atmosphere and location to the plot, was felt to be necessary. Lesser characters are usually commenting on the main characters' behaviour and actions. But because of this elimination the main characters have to exert themselves far more. They have to express a power and variety of meaning in a single or very few gestures whereas an actor often requires hundreds of words to explain his behaviour and actions.

However, beyond the similarity in construction, these works of Helpmann and Ashton are very different. If Fokine had been alive, he would surely have admired both works, designating Helpmann's *Hamlet* danced mime and Ashton's two ballets mimed dance of the subtlest kind (within the world of fantasy of *The Dream* or in the closely observed reality of the social world in *A Month in the Country*).

It should be placed on record that a complete outsider but lover of ballet, Sir Isaiah Berlin OM, suggested that music by Chopin would be suitable for Ashton's chosen subject, *A Month in the Country*. After much thought John Lanchbery arranged and orchestrated four little-known Chopin works to support and express Ashton's interpretation of the Turgenev comedy of manners. The *'La Ci Darem' Variations* became the heroine Natalia's theme. It displays some of the selfish irresponsibility shown in the Count's famous song in Mozart's *Don Giovanni*. The *Fantasy on Polish Airs* becomes the Tutor's theme and also sets the nationalistic style of *demi-caractère* dance (see pages 46 and 90) which includes elements of Polish dance idioms. The *Grande Polonaise* in E Flat serves to demonstrate that spontaneous burst into dance indulged in by both Russians and Poles when thoroughly elated. Lastly the *Andante Spinato* reveals the passions aroused between the young Tutor and Natalia when they finally submit to each other's embrace. That melody so wistful and sad ends Natalia's dream of love as she is left all alone (see page 56).

The works of other playwrights have inspired many choreographers. They include Strindberg's *Miss Julie*, Maeterlinck's *Pelléas and Mélisande* and *The Bluebird*, Garcia Lorca's *Las Hermanas*, Tennessee Williams' *A Streetcar Named Desire* and Ionescu's *A Young Man Must Marry* and *The Lesson*.

Poetry

Epic and other poetry have been another source of inspiration, particularly in the USSR where Pushkin is to every Russian what Shakespeare is to the English. Nowhere is love of his work shown more than in the twelve ballets and three operas inspired by his narrative poems. They are all highly dramatic or comic tales whose characters frequently belong to different peoples and social classes. The confrontations arising from the plot often give the choreographers ample scope to contrast one style of dance with another, as in *The Fountain of Bakhchisarai* (Polish and Tartar dance), and *The Prisoner in the Caucasus* (Russian Court and Georgian dance). It is the inclusion of this traditional material that makes such ballets seem so real to their audiences. But Russian choreographers have not chosen to turn the great Pushkin-Tchaikovsky operas of *Eugene Onegin* and *The Queen of Spades* into ballet as Cranko did with the former. This was explained by a Soviet friend as being impossible: 'Tchaikovsky made his music one with the words. It is the beauty of that collaboration which fills the heart and mind of our audiences to think of Pushkin's genius. The words without Tchaikovsky's music, or the music without the words would be meaningless.'

The above comment is of importance to would-be choreographers. If a choreographer has been inspired to incorporate words, then he should design movements which best express their meaning. There are two ways of doing this. Either they are interpreted literally, or the dancers comment upon them. Ashton has succeeded in using both methods. Few ballets arouse such laughter as *The Wedding Bouquet* (1937) where the speaker comments briefly and very much to the point, 'Josephine should not go to the wedding', as the lady in question sways drunkenly on the table and, 'Guy was a name that was spoken', as a supercilious and handsome guest breaks into a fairly spectacular solo. On the other hand, his interpretation of the Stravinsky-Gide *Persephone* (1961), with words spoken by Svetlana Beriosova or sung by the tenor representing the Greek chorus, brought the story vividly to life. The rhythmic expressive lilt of the words gave appropriate timing to the dance, expressing the moods, emotions and action of Persephone and the other characters.

MacMillan's interpretation of Mahler's *Song of the Earth* is similar in construction to Ashton's *Persephone* in that the choreographer allows the singers' words to dictate the movements. But he goes much further. Not only does he create movements to express the three main characters' moods, emotions and actions, but in some places he also describes the setting as in the lovely brief passage where the boys' bodies form the arches over the pond into which the girls are gazing. More importantly, he also makes comment on the philosophy underlying the Chinese poems of Life and Death, Youth and Age and always the renewal of life and hope (see also page 97).

There are other, important ballets inspired by music accompanying the songs of poets. Amongst the best known are Tudor's *Dark Elegies* to Mahler's music for *Kindertotenlieder* (songs on the death of children) by the German poet, Rückert, and Ashton's *Les Illuminations* to Benjamin Britten's music for poems by Rimbaud. By seeking to express not only the literal import of the words but also the philosophical thoughts behind them, the choreographers have given their audience a greater insight into their meaning. The examples quoted show how, when a ballet is being danced to words spoken or sung, it is essential that the gestures make sense and actually interpret or react to the words. If not, those sensitive to words will find the contradiction between words and gestures distracting and even disappointing.

Fiction

Several novels have sparked off interesting ballets, the best known being *Don Quixote* by Cervantes. It is impossible for any choreographer to retain the whole plot of this famous tale. Only de Valois (1950) came close to recapturing in a simple way the reality of some of the Don's fantasies as a chivalrous knight. Her solution to the problem of reconciling reality with fantasy was to make the village slut, Aldonza, serve him a drink at the village inn, pause and then to draw a long tress of black hair across her face, before turning to confront him as the Dulcinea of his dreams. This vision of a lady in distress sent him on his way to misadventures with his faithful squire and enormous steed. Although the music had been specially composed by Gerhard, few of its scenes allowed enough time for development of plot and character in sufficient depth. This was probably the reason for its lack of success. Yet there were several memorable passages, notably the beautiful classical *pas de deux* in the Don's vision of the Golden Age and the strange yet comic Descent into the Cave of Mont Cenis. The latter had an exciting frontcloth depicting the great shaft into which the Don and Sancho Panza gazed in fear before the old man descended. This and other designs were by Edward Burra. Few artists since the days of Diaghilev had contributed so much to create the proper setting and atmosphere for a ballet at once so realistic and so fantastic. Few who saw it will forget the other frontcloth which showed the long lanky Don precariously astride an enormous horse with Sancho Panza gazing upwards at the horse's hindquarters.

Episodes in Victor Hugo's *Notre-Dame de Paris* became *Esmeralda* in Petipa's hands but revealed its potential as a plot for ballet when Roland Petit staged his version. This owed much of its success to the influence of the first film version and Lon Chaney's famous portrayal of Quasimodo. Gogol's story of *Taras Bulba* and the Cossack uprising was given a faithful interpretation of the crude values and violence of real episodes in the history of the Ukraine. The choreographer Feodor Lopoukov made full use of the wide variety of folk dance in that area. It could not have been more different from Andrée Howard's *La Fête Etrange*. Her sensitive interpretation of a brief episode in Alain Fournier's *Le Grand Meaulnes* to some haunting music by Fauré told of the awakening love between a peasant boy and a young heiress when he strays into her garden. Andrée Howard showed the same sensitivity and understanding of subtle movement when she translated the strange novel by David Garnett, *Lady into Fox* (1939), into a ballet. She told it as if it were some frightening fairy tale of a fox transformed into a beautiful lady, who married the local squire but who was finally hunted and killed by hounds in full cry. These two ballets clearly showed how far choreographers had developed their means of expressive characterisation since Petipa's White Cat, Puss in Boots and Bluebirds in *The Sleeping Beauty* and Massine's poodles in *La Boutique Fantasque*. This style of animal choreography reached its peak when Ashton arranged his dances for the enchanting film, *The Tales of Beatrix Potter*.

Biography

Biographies do not seem to be a likely source of inspiration for ballet. Yet Eugene Loring picked on the life of a famous outlaw to create the first truly American ballet, *Billy the Kid* (1938). It reflected something of American film techniques such as flashbacks, swift cuts and occasional close-ups. MacMillan had already sought more widely in his efforts to portray real life in terms of dance. Four important works explore the working of the minds and the behaviour discussed by writers who have tried to explain their subject's actions and ways of living.

The first attempt at this difficult problem was *The Burrow* (1958) based on *The Diary of Anne Frank*, the Jewish girl who, after hiding with other refugees, was finally taken and murdered by the Nazis. In this work MacMillan shows how these refugees of

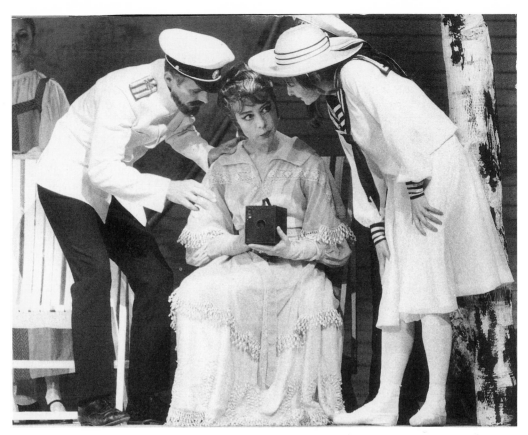

Anastasia   Above: youth and age – Anastasia at the naval review with her parents; below: age and experience – Anastasia trying to relive her past (Lynn Seymour, Svetlana Beriosova, Deryck Rencher; Lynn Seymour, David Adams)

all ages, types and temperaments react within their claustrophobic hiding place, their constant alertness and fear of discovery. When at last the sound of heavy footsteps in jackboots is heard and a shaft of light suddenly pierces the gloom, one knows exactly what is to be the fate of these tragic people. Few ballets have made so vehement a statement.

MacMillan followed *The Burrow* with *Anastasia*, which he had originally created as a one-act ballet (Berlin 1967), and enlarged it to three acts for London (1970). It told the story of Anastasia, the Tsar's youngest daughter, who perhaps escaped from the massacre of the Imperial family by the Bolsheviks. The first two acts are danced to music from Tchaikovsky's First and Third symphonies, which certainly create the atmosphere for the Imperial Court at the Naval review and at a ball in the Winter Palace of St. Petersburg before it is stormed by the revolutionaries. The last act, however, is danced to music by Martinu and finds Anastasia living in an asylum where past events are projected in film on the high walls of her room as if her life is flashing through her head as she sits on her bed rocking herself to and fro. This made every movement seem contorted by the agony of trying to recall past events. Whether the story is true or not, MacMillan's telling of it makes a powerful impression and convinces many in the audience that a portrayal of real life can be a subject for ballet.

MacMillan's next ballet from history was *Mayerling* (1978). This was another exercise in portraying the inner workings of the mind and resultant behaviour, in this case of Count Rudolf of Austria. The plot concerns Rudolf's affair with Mary Vetsera and their death. There are many conflicting opinions as to how the young couple died. Was it murder, suicide or both? Whatever the true cause, MacMillan gives his view of what happened and logical reasons for it. The result is a highly tragic ballet in which every member of the cast has to be a dancer-actor at every moment. At no point does the tension drop. This is due to the strong contrasts MacMillan makes between the movements of the half-deranged Rudolf and those of the women ordering his life. There is the cold and withdrawn Empress Mother whose love lies elsewhere; the terrified, prim Belgian princess, his newly wedded wife, who finally submits to his assault; and Mitzi, the cabaret dancer who freely exposes her charms to Rudolf and his fellow officers. There is also the distinctive style of the calculating Countess Larisch, one of Rudolf's ex-mistresses who contrives that he meet the beautiful Mary Vetsera. It is with the choreography for these two principal characters that MacMillan shows how fully he understands the mind of the beautiful young girl and her efforts to gain Rudolf's total commitment to herself. This is particularly noticeable in that she seems to go to any length, even to submitting herself to his brutal handling of her willing body. This ballet can be called a study in schizophrenia.

The same comment can perhaps be made of MacMillan's *Isadora* (1972), a study of an undisciplined, self-indulgent genius.

MacMillan has created other ballets in his search for plots based on real life. The most disturbing and horrific is *A Distant Drummer* (1984). This explains in explicit terms the bestialities of the Hitler regime and describes their effect on a simple soldier.

Opera

The examples of novels turned into ballets increase when one adds those which first became operas and then ballets at second hand. Outstanding are the many versions of

Mérimée's *Carmen*, sometimes but not always to Bizet's music. Roland Petit in his version did not always use this as Bizet intended. Many who knew the opera were disturbed by the way he switched what was essentially feminine music and gave it to a male character. The shock of seeing Don José dancing to Carmen's *Habanera* and Carmen dancing to his famous aria was too much. This is the danger of taking a well-known, even favourite, story and altering its substance whether it be plot or music.

Dumas' *La Dame aux Camélias* has also inspired several choreographers. It will certainly live on as Verdi's famous opera *La Traviata*, and perhaps in the memories of some balletgoers from Ashton's *Marguerite et Armand* (1963) to music by Liszt. It marked Nureyev's first appearance with Margot Fonteyn. Abbé Prévost's *Manon Lescaut* became Messager's opera and then MacMillan's ballet, *Manon*. Bellini's *La Sonnambula* (based on Scott's novel *The Bride of Lammermoor*) was an opera successfully translated into ballet by Balanchine.

Massine was tempted to interpret a Wagner opera, *Tristran and Isolde*, based on Celtic legend. His ballet was called *Tristan Fou* and with décor by Salvador Dali lived up to the title.

Operettas have proved a richer source of inspiration to choreographers than opera. This is possibly because these light-hearted works contain so much danceable music. Massine's *Madame Angot* and Ashton's *The Two Pigeons* are amongst them.

Cranko's *Pineapple Poll* is the real gem in this genre as far as England is concerned. It conveys the truly irreverent spirit and gusty humour of the very English operas of Gilbert and Sullivan. It is directly based on one of Gilbert's Bab Ballads with music by Sullivan selected by Charles Mackerras and woven by him into a truly nautical score for Cranko's choreography. This was rightly called 'Variations on a Hornpipe Theme' by Edwin Evans. Cranko made use of several favourite ploys of the English music halls and pantomime – as did Gilbert in his librettos. There is the delicious sight of the heroine Poll and the sailors' wives masquerading as 'jolly tars' and making every conceivable mistake when performing deck or gun drill. There is also a rousing Finale when the Bride's garrulous aunt is hoisted aloft as Britannia draped in the Union Jack and using her umbrella as the shield. At one performance the Frenchman sitting at my side was appalled: 'We cannot do that to our Marianne.' Whereupon my nephew retorted: 'What a pity!', and tried vainly to explain why the English can always make fun of their most cherished institutions – even their Navy.

It is a point would-be choreographers should consider. Each nation has its own sense of humour, comedy and ways of laughter-making. Whatever makes an English audience laugh seldom gets the same response elsewhere unless it is simply straight-forward fun.

Painting

Despite the importance of artists who have designed sets and costumes for ballet, few choreographers have bothered to explore other artists' work as a source of inspiration. De Valois' *The Rake's Progress* (1935) based on Hogarth's famous paintings still holds the audience's attention. Hogarth painted these as a comment on the social ills of his time and de Valois fully captured their spirit and atmosphere. She worked out her choreography as she had done for *Job* (see page 24) so that the sorry tale unfolds in a flowing series of pictures in dance that strictly follow the lines drawn by Hogarth. During the 1939–45 War she was inspired by the cartoonist Rowlandson, who, like Hogarth, was adept at pointing out the ills and abuses of his time. The *Prospect Before Us* brought to life in hilarious fashion the problems of the London theatres during the eighteenth century when rival managers stole each other's balletmasters and dancers, were often on strike and saw their theatres burnt to the ground or the workers fighting each other. This light-hearted look at the history of the theatre was a real tonic to audiences during the Blitz. It aroused such laughter that when they emerged to encounter fires raised by the bombs, the real scene only seemed a continuation of what they had just seen, for the frontcloth, after Rowlandson, depicted the Theatre Royal, Drury Lane, on fire.

One aspect of choreography which can be influenced by a study of painting is evident in MacMillan's *Requiem*. Much of the beauty and expressive line of his choreography for this moving work lies in the eloquent *ports de bras* of all the performers. Most of these come from his study of Blake's paintings. In some cases, he has used Blake's own tiny changes in the angles of wrists and fingers; whilst the dancers' bodies either move onwards or remain static, their heads suddenly look upwards in joy after being cast down in grief. Would-be choreographers would do well to study what differences can be made in the simplest step to demonstrate how a body heavily laden with sorrow can suddenly be lightened by a gleam of hope. In MacMillan's *The Burrow* (see page 30), the dancers in one single movement express despair as the shaft of light comes through the doorway. In *Requiem* the change from downward to upward movement expresses pure joy.

It has already been noted how Ashton was inspired by Renaissance paintings when creating *The Wise Virgins* (see page 24). They were a source for one of Rambert's earliest works: it was a Botticelli Madonna in *A Florentine Picture*. De Valois also created an interesting reconstruction of Manet's *Bar aux Folies Bergère* for the Rambert Ballet. This was a tiny masterpiece of observation and imagination which seemed to say, 'Who is she serving?' The exercise of observing and imagining what would happen if a picture came to life is something that would-be choreographers should adopt. There are so many art galleries containing valuable pictures. Degas was not the only painter of dance. (Many attempts have been made to bring his work to life.) Perhaps one day someone will attempt a choreographic design based on one of Breughel's many pictures, particularly his *Children's Games*.

Pastimes and games

When a choreographer wishes to make a statement about pastimes and games, the field is enormous. But there are limitations in the sense that once the subject has been chosen, every movement made by the dancers has to explore the way it is performed in real life. This will often involve all parts of the body and the rhythm and tempo of the appropriate gestures.

Ashton's *Les Patineurs* (1937) is an ever-popular ballet of this kind and shows the antics on the ice of various types of skaters. It requires a highly disciplined group of dancers if its expertise is to be fully conveyed.

But one had to go to Nijinska's *Le Train Bleu* (1924) to appreciate how it was possible to depict a sophisticated wealthy clientele disporting themselves on the Riviera. This was the first of Diaghilev's so-called contemporary ballets. It reflected exactly its period and how such people enjoyed their fashionable beach sports. Their clothes were designed by Chanel, at that time the great arbiter of fashion.

This ballet could not have been more different from Gore's *Street Games* (1943) where grubby children play in a slum street. Hopscotch, skipping, jumping over the rope and a game of tag all find a place.

Balanchine's *Card Game* (1956) (later re-worked by Cranko, 1962) is an essay in yet another field of games, but in no way resembles de Valois' *Checkmate* (1935). The latter is not a ballet with a theme; it has a highly dramatic plot. The difference between the two works explains how difficult it is to classify many twentieth-century ballets into one particular category. The game of poker played in Balanchine and Cranko's work has its rules, so does chess, and the three choreographers show their knowledge

Checkmate A ballet inspired by games: the Black Queen is trapped (June Highwood, Roland Price)

Checkmate   A ballet inspired by games: the Red King loses his crown (Margaret Barbieri, David Bintley)

of the necessary deals or moves. But neither version of *Card Game* suggests that there is much conflict. The climax is probably when the Joker disports himself, particularly in Cranko's version where he dons a tutu. *Checkmate* has a proper beginning, climax and end (see page 56). First comes the mustering of the red pieces. The resultant play rises to the climax as the Black Queen confronts, fights and ultimately kills the Red Knight. It ends with the black pieces encircling the Red King and trapping him in their staves so that the Black Queen can seize his crown and stab him to death.

PART 2
BALLETIC MATERIALS

Having been inspired to create a ballet by any one of the sources mentioned, choreographers have to decide upon the appropriate materials with which to work. The most important are music and the type of dancer.

Music

Music must be chosen that will best give the overall and phrase rhythms to the steps, poses and gestures, that will help to create the atmosphere and mood of the whole and that will underline the action. Alternatively, the choreographer may be inspired by a piece of music and wish to bring it to life in dance (see page 41). There are three types of music from which to choose.

Specially commissioned music

From the first *ballets de cour* until the beginning of the twentieth century music was always specially commissioned. Much of the music played by a pianist for ballet lessons is still borrowed from the dance suites of court, opera and other ballets of the eighteenth and nineteenth centuries, as well as from other dance suites of Bach, Mozart, Beethoven and Brahms. Most items in these suites were designed to contrast one with another by varied time signatures, tempi and phrasing so that they built up to a climax which, in the early days, signalled the entrance of the king or the most important participant. Each dance followed particular rules laid down by the dancing masters, and this idea continued to prevail even after Gluck began to compose operas and ballets which had greater continuity. His ideas of symphonic development were followed by Beethoven (*Prometheus* 1801), Adam (*Giselle* 1841), Delibes (*Coppélia* 1870) and Tchaikovsky. Although the scores of *The Sleeping Beauty* and *The Nutcracker* followed Petipa's explicit orders that each item consisted of so many bars of one tempo and time signature and as to what it was supposed to represent, Tchaikovsky did demonstrate how ballet music could be developed symphonically by using the leitmotifs. He showed how music could flow through a scene and not be broken up into short numbers which encouraged the audience to applaud each time.

Stravinsky composed the first truly modern score for ballet with *The Firebird* (see page 61). He understood that there must be an overall rhythm as well as the phrase rhythms of particular leitmotifs and dances if dancers were to understand and feel properly Fokine's choreographic design. Stravinsky confessed that he borrowed the idea from Tchaikovsky and his own example was followed by later composers of specially commissioned scores.

Amongst the most important of these carefully plotted works are: de Falla's *The Three-Cornered Hat* (1919) which originally accompanied a mime play and so fascinated Diaghilev that he commissioned the composer to enlarge it for Massine's ballet (see page 59); Vaughan William's *Job*, commissioned by Diaghilev, was unused until de Valois created her important 'Masque for Dancing' (1931) (this marked the inaugural performance of what has become The Royal Ballet); Arthur Bliss' *Checkmate* (1937) was choreographed by de Valois after both composer and choreographer had worked on the plot; Prokofiev's *Romeo and Juliet* was composed with the help of a Shakespearean theatre expert and has been used notably by Lavrovsky, Ashton and MacMillan (see page 26); and Ashton provided a roughly outlined plot for Hans Werner Henze's score for *Ondine* (1958).

But standing out above all are the scores commissioned from Stravinsky by Balanchine, such as *Apollo*, *Orpheus* and *Card Game*.

During the third phase of his enterprise Diaghilev realised the need to keep up with the tastes of his wealthy audiences always anxious to be in fashion and commissioned works from members of the group known as Les Six. These were Milhaud, Poulenc and Auric whose music greatly influenced many later composers such as William Walton and Constant Lambert, many of their works remain in constant use today as witness MacMillan's moving interpretation of Poulenc's *Gloria*.

When choreographers decide to commission music, they should first give the composer an outline of the plot, roughly suggesting the sequence of the action, the likely entrances and exits for the characters and the dances or brief scenes in which they are involved. Secondly, some description should be given of the characters, their moods, emotions and particular role in each part of the action. Thirdly, it may be valuable to indicate the style or quality of the movements to be used. Fourthly, the choreographer should indicate roughly how long each dance or episode should last. It cannot be repeated too often that a dancer requires less time to make a statement than do words or music. No matter how interesting the music and the dance movements, if the passages are too long the dancer rarely has sufficient stamina to sustain the dance to its proper climax. This happened in Benjamin Britten's *The Prince of the Pagodas* and, originally, in the Red Knight's dance in *Checkmate* (Arthur Bliss later shortened it, giving it much greater strength and significance).

Specially arranged music

'Specially Arranged Music' refers to those scores where a musician, in collaboration with a choreographer, selects from the varied works of a particular composer and weaves them into a viable ballet score.

After Diaghilev's death composers seemed reluctant to create what Edwin Evans said they called 'accompaniments to dance', because they 'preferred to create the new for the sake of being new'. Their efforts certainly often lacked the rhythm and phrasing suitable for interpretation by physical and not mechanical means. It was then that choreographers turned their attention to music already available, very often because financial difficulties prevented any approach being made to a living composer. Since 1933, and the development of recording, there has been an immense range of both well- and little-known music on which to build all kinds of ballet (see page 56). But this will be to no avail if the choreographer is attempting to tell a story and does not have expert advice from musicians of the calibre of Edwin Evans, Constant Lambert

La Fille Mal Gardée   Ashton's English comic masterpiece
The Cock and Hens squawk in their roost (The Royal Ballet)

and John Lanchbery. All made valuable scores from existing music for de Valois, Ashton and MacMillan. Not all the results were of the same high quality; nevertheless the music they arranged reinforced the choreographer's design by giving the plot atmosphere, local colour, continuity and flow as well as giving the dancing its rhythmic vitality, emotion and mood. In some cases it also helped to underline the main moments in the action by emphasising gestures for greater strength and expression. In other cases they added humour, most notably in Lanchbery's score for *La Fille Mal Gardée*, where several witty slants in the orchestration raise laughter, for example the music for the Cock and the Hens.

However, music chosen from a composer's total output and specially arranged as a score for a three-act ballet with a story has rarely been completely successful. The composer wrote the song, piano solo, quartet or whatever for a particular purpose and for particular soloists, groups of musicians or an orchestra. He could not anticipate that his work would be put to an entirely different use, let alone tell a story. Two contrasting examples of what can happen when music is borrowed are Tomassini's arrangement of Scarlatti's sparkling music for Massine's *The Good-Humoured Ladies* and the arrangement of the same composer's music for Cranko's *The Taming of the Shrew* which merely gives overall and rough phrase rhythms as time-keepers for a three-act ballet.

On the other hand, Charles Mackerras' wonderful pot-pourri of tunes from the Gilbert and Sullivan operas for *Pineapple Poll* displayed how well he has caught not only the humour but also the pathos of The Bum Boat Woman's Story. Choreographers should also study John Lanchbery's sensitive handling of some lesser-known Chopin music for Ashton's *A Month in the Country* and his equally successful score for Ashton's film, *The Tales of Beatrix Potter*. He based the latter on his research into Victorian and Edwardian 'salon' music and showed what can be done by looking into such highways and byways of music when a particular period atmosphere is needed. The same can be said about Constant Lambert's arrangement of Auber's music for Ashton's *Les Rendezvous* and Meyerbeer's for Ashton's *Les Patineurs*.

Specially chosen music

'Specially Chosen Music' refers to particular pieces of music that have inspired a choreographer and whose score has been interpreted by the choreographer as it stands, the composer's scheme and continuity unchanged.

In 1901, Gorsky was inspired by Glinka's *Valse Fantaisie* to create the first abstract ballet. His example was followed by Fokine with *Les Sylphides* (music by Chopin) and *Le Carnaval* (music by Schumann).

It was when Colonel de Basil re-started Diaghilev's Ballets Russes that his major choreographers, Massine, and later, Balanchine, turned their attention to the symphonies, concertos, chamber and other music by composers such as Tchaikovsky (Fifth Symphony for *Les Présages*), Brahms (Fourth Symphony for *Choreartium*), Beethoven (Seventh Symphony for *Seventh Symphony*), Mozart (music for *Mozartiana*) and Bach (Double Violin Concerto for *Double Concerto*).

Major composers have continued to provide an abundant source of inspiration to more recent choreographers. They have not always been as humble as Balanchine in submitting to the dictates of the score as envisaged by the composer. This can be of particular significance if the chosen music is already combined with words, either sung or spoken. Fine examples of this kind are MacMillan's *Song of the Earth* and Ashton's *Persephone* and *The Wedding Bouquet*. In the last example, the words form frivolous comment on the action. But there is no such careful blending of ingredients in Tetley's *Dances of Albion* where the singer's words of the traditional 'Lye Wake Dirge' bore no relation to what was being danced on stage. This was offensive to the Scots in the audience as was Tetley's disregard for the purport of the poem by Blake that gave the ballet its title. The music by Benjamin Britten includes some part of the War Requiem which means far more to British audiences than mere decorative patterning.

Choreographers have never disdained to use popular music for their ever-increasing audiences and they realise that they should reflect popular taste. The score for *La Fille Mal Gardée* (1789) reflected the new revolutionary ideas pervading France and contained several folk and popular airs. This example was followed by Gavin Gordon, singer-composer, who borrowed street songs and cries for his score of *The Rake's Progress*.

Audiences today expect choreographers to satisfy current demands. The influence of jazz and Latin American rhythms caught the attention of Les Six, Walton and Lambert and in turn inspired choreographers such as Ashton. He used music by Walton and words by Edith Sitwell for *Façade*. (He was later to commission Richard

Rodney Bennett to provide a score for his *Jazz Calendar* based on the old nursery rhyme 'Monday's child'.) Balanchine created a ballet *The Seven Deadly Sins* with music by Kurt Weill and words by Berthold Brecht which later inspired MacMillan to stage his version of this parable for the times. Music by Scott Joplin then helped him to create his light-heartedly comic *Elite Syncopations*.

Would-be choreographers have an enormous field from which to seek inspiration. It ranges from the traditional dances of ancient Greece used by David Bintley for his *Choros* to the latest pieces of minimal music by John Cage that are used for Robbins' *Glass Pieces*.

Musically inspired ballets

Choreographers wishing to interpret music in dance terms are limited in several ways because their choice should not only determine the style of dance used and its phrasing but other factors which are an integral part of the score. Their task is nowhere better summed up than by Ernest Newman, one of the great music critics of his day, who rarely watched ballet until intrigued by the news that Massine was creating ballets to Tchaikovsky's Fifth Symphony (*Les Présages*, London 1933) and to Brahms' Fourth Symphony (*Choreartium*, London 1933). Newman was overwhelmed by the latter and wrote in *The Sunday Times*: 'Strictly speaking no art is translatable into another, not even poetry into music. The most we can get is convincing parallelisms between the two and the fact that some parallelisms are much more difficult than others and have hitherto not been attempted is no reason for denying that a choreographic genius like Massine has the right to attempt this. Massine has given a translation into choreographic terms of a hundred musical features of the Symphony. The ballet works itself out consistently as a design, reproducing in the subtlest way the design of the music in the matter of subject, repetitions, balancings, treatment of episodes and so on. In the last resort, the more musical we are and the better we know Brahms, the more pleasure we derive from *Choreartium*.'

Ernest Newman's remarks stress that choreographers creating dance to their own choice of music must study how the composer has structured his score and try to understand what he intended the audience to hear and feel, whether it be played, or played and sung. Choreographers have to create dance movements which make their response to the music visible before the performers can communicate the music. A so-called abstract or dance ballet has to be both thought and felt if the partnership between the often-dead composer and the living interpreters is to make sense. It is perhaps worth recording the remark of an eight-year-old boy on first seeing Ashton's *Symphonic Variations* (1947): 'That was lovely, I know all about the music now. The dancers told me.'

The remark could only be made because Ashton had given so much thought to how the music could be given shape in dance. There are three aspects which have to be considered in all dance interpretations of music. Firstly, the style used should reflect something of the period and quality of the chosen score; secondly, the dance should reveal something of its technical construction; thirdly, the movements should parallel the composer's treatment and development of the various episodes and the orchestration. Some guidance on how to achieve these aspects of interpretation can be gained by a study of ballets by Ashton, Fokine, MacMillan and others. The examples are not always abstract ballets, because the three aspects described above are applicable to most choreography if music and dance are to be equal partners in a ballet.

How Ashton reflects the period and quality of the music

A study of five Ashton ballets shows that all are based on classical technique, despite their apparent differences. Each reflects something of the period and quality of the music, the period being of the time when written by the composer or when presented as a ballet and the quality being that inspired in the choreographer by the composer.

Symphonic Variations (1947)

Sir Neville Cardus, another great music critic writing about the history of music, likened the image of great composers such as Bach, Mozart and Beethoven as, 'Looking at a range of mountains, those names are on the summits then one comes to a plateau – and there standing out and rising from it is the cathedral of César Franck.' This statement exactly sums up the quality and feeling of Franck's music. As organist and piano teacher most of it was composed for performance at some ritual, often in church – it conveys not only the solemnity of the occasion but also the spaciousness of the building and the sound of the organ with its vast range of tonalities. It is without emotion but conveys a sense of reverence for order and serenity. Although *Symphonic Variations* was not intended as a ritual, Ashton can be said to have used it as such for six dancers who were practising their art in the spacious simplicity of Sophie Fedorovitch's décor. But it was and is something more. Those first six dancers had come to celebrate the newly awakened school of English classical dance that was establishing itself with the coming of peace. Like Franck's music, Ashton's dance flows onwards in simple lines and phrases, each one is of equal value to the whole, neither pianist, nor orchestra, nor dancers indulge in virtuoso passages which would destroy the solemn serenity of the design.

Symphonic Variations
Ashton's definition of English classical dance in 1947 (The Royal Ballet)

Scènes de Ballet (1954)

Ashton's *Scènes de Ballet* could not be more different from the previous example. Stravinsky was commissioned to provide the score for a New York revue, 1944 (choreography by Anton Dolin). He undoubtedly had in mind the particular patterns and balanced relationship of the various dances (i.e. solos, *grands pas*, *variations*, etc.) as laid out in all Petipa ballets and he made the ballerina the focus of all attention. Ashton punctiliously followed the layout. But Stravinsky's music, although classical in form, was far from the tuneful dance idioms of Tchaikovsky, Stravinsky's source of inspiration. Despite strict rhythm and exact phrasing, the music was daringly frivolous in tone and quality because it was meant to entertain a popular audience. In following Stravinsky's guidelines, Ashton found many new, sometimes frivolous, ways of performing class-room steps. The *corps de ballet* neglect the turn-out and step forwards *sur les pointes*, raising the working knee and resting the toe on the calf of the other leg, before moving forwards. They travel forwards instead of *en place* in *échappé relevés* after breaking the rule that the arms never cross the centre line of the body and are always (except in *arabesque*) rounded. If Ashton's *Scènes de Ballet* is compared with Balanchine's *Ballet Imperial*, it will be seen that Balanchine rarely breaks away from the classical technique as practised in Petipa's day when Tchaikovsky wrote the music. Ashton, like Stravinsky, took into account the technical developments which had taken place. Petipa's orders to Tchaikovsky were sacrosanct because the composer knew that if that 'dictator' did not approve the music would have to be changed (as it was for *The Nutcracker*). Although studying and admiring Tchaikovsky's methods of composition, Stravinsky felt he could break away from the stereotyped dance forms demanded by nineteenth-century balletmasters. His music was far more economical in melody and orchestral sound but his rhythmic phrasings and marked attention to newer dance forms inspired Ashton to break away from traditional class-room practices.

Birthday Offering (1956)

Ashton's third classical ballet *Birthday Offering* to music by Glazounov was a celebration of the twenty-fifth birthday of The Royal Ballet and of the seven ballerinas it had now fostered. Ashton resorted to Petipa's way of selecting and phrasing the steps, poses and *ports de bras* which would best display the ballerinas' individual qualities. It was a celebration of their talents because, by being confined – so to speak – to those steps which they most enjoyed and thus performed best, they positively sparkled. Different dancers have to work hard both technically and as individuals to bring out the particular qualities which Ashton saw in the original performers. Nevertheless, the design comes directly from the traditional vocabulary and, with thought, it can be performed by dancers who possess strong and precise technique and who can enjoy the challenge it sets before them.

Monotones I and II (1965)

Erik Satie, like César Franck, was an organist and piano teacher. He composed much liturgical music but he admitted that, in writing his *Gymnopédies* and *Gnossiennes* for the entertainment of his friends, he had been vaguely inspired by the friezes on antique Greek vases. This was the clue upon which Ashton based his fourth classical ballet, *Monotones I and II*. Each finds a trio of dancers working close together to form

Monotones II   Ashton's sense of linear design (The Royal Ballet)

and re-form beautiful groupings as they weave their patterns over the stage in softly projected shafts of light. There are calm, spaciousness and perfectly balanced pictures within the overall design which from time to time acquire a more athletic quality, particularly in *Monotones II* (i.e. two boys and a girl). This forming and re-forming of pictures never loses its serenity. It resembles the pictures of dancers frozen for all time by the potters who made the Greek vases just to display their feats. Ashton's dancers have to weave themselves into and out of such play without losing the flow of both music and movement.

Rhapsodie (1982)

Ashton's fifth dance ballet is different again (see also page 54). In it he expressed his own and his dancers' sheer enjoyment of 'just dancing to music which cries out to be danced'. That passionate love of 'music as movement' is what Rachmaninov's *Rhapsody on a Theme of Paganini* is all about. To have heard Rachmaninov play his own or any other Russian music or to listen to his orchestral works is to realise he was a passionate musician, loving his art and giving his all to express the joys and sorrows, the tender and brutal moods and all the emotions to which man is subject. In composing the *Rhapsody*, Rachmaninov tried to vary the Paganini theme as much as possible by differentiating the instrumental sections one from another. Whereas *Symphonic Variations* flows onwards in simple serenity, Ashton, following Rachmaninov, here uses an enormous variety of steps and constantly changes the choreographic phrasing to reflect the increasing or diminishing sounds and to match the tempi of the melody, in order to give his *enchaînements* light and shade and to indicate the sheer complexity of the orchestration. That he was so successful was not because his dancers were technical experts, but because he made them feel Rachmaninov's passionate love of 'music as movement'.

Dance rhythm
(see also pages 41 and 68)

'Every dance has its own rhythm.' This is the very first idea to be taken into consideration when a choreographer starts to work with music. He should remember that most ballet music until that of Tchaikovsky was based on the same time signatures, tempi and phrasing as that of fashionable court and, later, social dances i.e. waltzes, polkas, galops, minuets, gavottes, mazurkas and so on. Tchaikovsky was the first to break that mould when he gave the Sapphire Fairy (now one of Florestan's sisters) a solo to a 5/4 time signature. But this was only innovative in so far as classical ballet was concerned as there are many 5/4 Slav folk dances. Ashton makes brilliant use of this in his version of the solo, phrasing the steps so that a jump upwards can last three beats followed by two short steps or two beats followed by a long and then a short step. Taking time in the air makes leaps appear higher and more sustained than is usual.

Music should, however, not be used merely as a time-keeper as the above remarks may suggest. Choreographers should understand that counting beats or what is called the measure of the music is not dance rhythm. The time signature is merely a guide to the number of minims, crotchets and quavers there are in a bar. (The first note is usually the longest and marks the beginning.) Dance rhythm means how the varying lengths of notes are grouped together within a phrase. Briefly, it is how the composer, like the author of a sentence or of a line in a poem, groups his 'words' in order of importance so that they make sense. The choreographer can make an overall rhythm for a long phrase of music and within it shorter phrases.

This is well exemplified in Fokine's choreography for the first Nocturne in *Les Sylphides*, where it can be said that the *corps de ballet* are marking the overall rhythm lasting sixteen or thirty-two bars, whilst the three soloists represent the shorter rhythmical phrases lasting four to eight bars. Ashton does something similar in *Symphonic Variations* where he makes overall phrase rhythms from *pas de burrée en place* accompanied by very distinctive *ports de bras*. These are marked by three of the dancers whilst another performs a solo to a short phrase. In this case three girls interpret the very rhythmic orchestral accompaniment whilst the male soloist interprets the shorter melodic phrase played by the pianist. In both these examples Fokine and Ashton are following Ivanov's choreography for the beautiful Act II *pas de deux* in *Swan Lake*. In it the *corps de ballet* frequently mark the overall rhythmic beat whilst Odette and Siegfried dance to the melody played by solo violin and 'cello. Another equally interesting way of marking the rhythmic beat occurs in Fokine's *Carnaval* when Columbine dances to the semi-quavers and Harlequin to the quavers as they enter side by side.

A further study of *Les Sylphides* reveals Fokine's great understanding of the dance rhythms which he felt he had to make visible whenever he was using well-recognised dance forms. For example, in the solo waltz the dancer marks the three beats of a waltz in roughly every other bar, usually with her feet, but in the third musical phrase she poses in *arabesque* and marks the beat by gradually lowering her hand three times. The accent throughout the dance is lightly marked on the first beat. However, in the two mazurkas, Fokine expected the dancers slightly to accent the second beat of each bar as in any traditional mazurka or polonaise.

This is something that Ashton emphasises when Natalia, Kolia, Vera and the Tutor dance to Chopin's *Grande Polonaise* and *Fantasy on Polish Airs* in *A Month in the Country*. It is this careful attention to traditional dance rhythms which is so important to the style of both ballets, although neither can be called a character or national work (see page 28). Choreographers can make subtle differences between dancing to a waltz, mazurka or polonaise and there are contrasting rhythms to be found in a 3/4 time signature. Another way of accenting it is the so-called *à six temps*, that is, two bars with six strong beats. This was a favourite rhythm for male solos used particularly by nineteenth-century balletmasters. Changes can be made in the look of any step not by a change in the tempo but in the time signature: for example, dancing a *pas de basque* to a 2/4 or 6/8 instead of the usual 3/4.

The rise and fall of the melody

Fokine wanted to make dance rhythm visible by more than just marking the beats. He felt that if he waltzed his dancers round and round as in a ballroom he would not be interpreting Chopin's idealised romantic waltzes for a solo pianist. Such a performance would not be theatrically viable. His design had to reveal the pattern and phrasing of the dream world he wished to conjure up. He followed Ivanov's example in Act II of *Swan Lake* in which Odette's movements rise and fall with the melody. Something that Ashton does in most of his ballets.

In *Requiem*, MacMillan goes further. He was using a modern style of movement therefore the rise and fall of his design had far greater dimensions and therefore greater emotional content. His dancers had to parallel the sonorities of Fauré's solemn ritual of mourning. From the opening piteous pleas with shaking hands as the dancers sink to the floor in the depths of their sorrow, the choreographic pattern of the overall rhythm is seen to swell in size and intensity as the music does until there comes the gleam of hope, a quiet moment when a child-like figure dances in wonder at the ways in which she can explore not only the space in which she moves, but also the ways in which she shapes each part of her body into an ever flowing design. The dancers and music then swell to fill the stage again, ultimately to depart all sorrow spent with the child-like figure lifted high in the hands of one man and carried away out of sight whilst another dancer kneels low in homage as the music resolves the picture into a great Amen.

Further examples of musical interpretation

There are other ways in which choreographers can be guided by the musical context other than those already cited. When inspired by Tchaikovsky's Fifth Symphony to create *Les Présages* (1933), Massine took a theme which proposed that Man would win his struggle against Fate if he had Action, Love and Frivolity on his side. The moods and emotions of each were expressed in the first three movements. In the fourth, Man, with the help of the three soloists from the other movements, overcame the bat-like figure representing Fate. Massine took this theme from Tchaikovsky's own letters to his patron in which he described a composer's search for ideas. Similarly Massine interpreted Berlioz's own synopsis for the *Symphonie Fantastique*. This told how the poet, having taken opium, dreamt backwards through time to seek his love in a ballroom, on his way to a medieval scaffold, at a well in ancient Greece and finally at a Witches' Sabbath, where her kiss ended in death (see page 56).

However, Massine's interpretation of Brahms' Fourth Symphony (*Choreartium*, 1933) was very different. It was the ideas behind this design that so interested not only the audience but also the music critics of the time (see page 41). Massine not only paralleled the overall and short phrase rhythms of the music by those of the dancers, but the instruments of the orchestra by related groups of dancers. Each group was led by a soloist representing the leader of a particular orchestral section so that as the themes were taken up by first one and then another section, the various groups of dancers joined in. This is most obvious in the fourth movement, the Passacaglia or set of variations. The musical theme is initially stated by all the instruments playing a series of eight chords. Massine interprets these chords by setting six dancers about the stage and on each chord the six men either singly or together, and in turn, rise into a *tour en l'air* finishing in a *pose*. The *tour* is repeated, as are the chords, at the beginning of each variation which features a different orchestral section and its accompanying set of dancers. As these related groups are active throughout, both the musical content and its orchestration are made visible. It is this relationship which led to Ernest Newman's remark that, 'The ballet was living music' (see page 41).

The same critic's remark that Massine had captured the essence of Brahms' Fourth Symphony by 'repetitions, balancing and treatment of episodes' should be clarified. By repetition, he did not mean that every time a phrase was repeated it had to be the same. On the contrary, he also asserted that it needed variation. For example, the six male dancers do not always appear in the same place nor end in the same pose in the passages mentioned above. No! Massine followed Petipa's example of the solos by Aurora and the Six Fairies in *The Sleeping Beauty*. They may repeat the same step but the *ports de bras* or *épaulement* may change at each repeat. Petipa and Massine also met Newman's requirement for the balancing and treatment of episodes. This is perhaps best understood by the way both choreographers frequently show that certain steps can be danced *sur les pointes* but can also be jumped, e.g. *petits changements* or *sissonnes piquées*. Whichever way they are danced they must be set so that the one step grows logically out of the other because the music and the dancer have become excited by their relationship as the dance unfolds. This is what must happen when a ballet ends happily. Three fine examples of this exhilaration can be found in the excited circling of the cast round the hero and heroine in such ballets as *Coppélia*, *Pineapple Poll* and *Daphnis and Chloë*.

Choreographers however should avoid what can be called a purely technical analysis of the music by matching particular patterns of steps to particular musical phrases whenever they appear. This is what Balanchine has frequently done. It was first noted in *Ballet Imperial* (1941) when every time a scale-like passage in the second movement of Tchaikovsky's Piano Concerto No. 2 is played, the three soloists link hands to make two arches through which the *corps de ballet* 'ran round the houses' (Edwin Evans). This type of device is repeated again and again in other works whose music contains similar passages. Other easily recognised Balanchine signatures

Daphnis and Chloë Ashton's Romantic style
The Lovers are united (Margot Fonteyn, Christopher Gable and The Royal Ballet)

can be seen in passages marked *Stretto* where his dancers stab their toes into the floor as they travel across the stage in *posés attitudes devant* or *à la seconde*. Some choreographers today have adopted the same habit. For example, when the musical phrases get complicated because of the use of many notes, the dancers find themselves using their hands feverishly in order to give every note its value. Occasionally this can be interesting as it is in Bintley's *Consort Lessons* (1984). But if it is repeated too often the incessant jigging of hands makes the audience restless, too. A study of Dalcroze Eurythmics from which such ideas emanate is valuable, but the practice must be used with discretion if the resultant ballet is not to resemble an examination of machinery rather than a feeling for the rhythm and shape of the engine that makes the dancers perform.

It is often not understood by outsiders that certain types of music immediately suggest to dancers, teachers and choreographers particular kinds of steps. The 'insiders' can walk down the corridors of the National schools in London, Leningrad, Paris, Moscow, Copenhagen, Milan and elsewhere, pause to listen outside a studio door and know instantly what type of step is being practised. For example, it is necessary to hear only a brief phrase of some Grand Waltz by Tchaikovsky, Glinka or Strauss to know that steps of *grande élévation* are the object of the exercise; to hear some slow pavane, minuet or saraband is to realise that an *adage* is being practised. Choreographers, like dancers, have long memories and what a student experiences in a class-room can trigger off an idea much later. What develops may and usually does have some similarity to what was danced as a student. Characteristic qualities of a step are likely to be retained because the type of music so decrees, although it will rarely be identical in its performance because it will have been refurbished.

Types of dancer

Having chosen the story, theme or music, choreographers must consider the available living material through which they can mould the particular style of dance appropriate to their ideas. It is well known that they always develop their more satisfying choreographic ideas when working with a group of dancers whose abilities they know. It is then easier to select the individuals best suited to the proposed task. This is the case regardless of whether they take an objective, subjective or general view of their work (see page 62). The selection of dancers is also made easier because dancers fall roughly into four categories (see page 51) which are determined by individual characteristics and abilities. Training will have made dancers more adept at a certain style of dance and they usually show preference for a certain type of step: elevation, *pointe* work, *pirouettes* or whatever. Another characteristic of importance to the choreographer is the nature of a dancer's response to music.

As stated earlier, whereas creative artists such as authors commit words to paper, artists paint or carve and composers write scores away from the performers, choreographers create movements directly on the dancers in front of them. Although it is now possible to use a system of notation, choreographers still prefer to create directly on the human material, working on it and relying on the dancers' own memories to repeat what has been designed on and for them. Choreographers should, therefore, remember that dancers possess physical and mental abilities of their own which should be used effectively and expressively. Choreographers must have been dancers themselves if they are to understand and feel the natural abilities of the body and to allow for the influence of the techniques in which they have been trained. In addition they have to appreciate that all movement is affected by moods, emotions and actions. Only by such understanding can a ballet be created with style and expression.

Despite what some modern choreographers seem to believe, the human body has certain well-defined limitations beyond which it is not possible to go, no matter how hard the choreographers push their intellectual ideas. Dance is a physical manifestation and dancers only become expressive when they can feel the movements both physically and emotionally, and when they are inspired by the choreographer's interpretation and enthusiasm.

It is widely recognised that the classical technique can and does prove a stable basis for all styles of dance. Dancing masters gradually developed the classical technique from European folk dance which they first changed into the elegant steppings of courtiers in the palaces of Italian and Spanish kings and prelates. The technique was further refined by Italian dancing masters employed by the French kings whose courts became the richest in Europe. It was increasingly polished during the reign of Louis XIV when the first professional dancers took over from the courtiers after the founding of the Académie Royale de Danse within the Académie Royale de Musique (1672). This early style of classical dance displayed the talents of each particular performer, therefore many rules were laid down in order to achieve perfection of movement. These rules were based on the knowledge of what movements the dancers' bodies were capable.

Canon Arbeau in his *Orchésographie* (1588) recommended the use of four positions from and through which the feet moved, the turn-out to show off the line of the leg and *ports de bras* to display one's carriage and courteous behaviour. John Weaver, dancing master of Shrewsbury Grammar School, went further. He wrote the first textbook on the relationship between the natural functions of the bones, ligaments, tendons and muscles, and dance movement. His *Anatomical and Mechanical Lectures on Dancing* (1723) described the four movements 'of which the body is capable', namely: to bend, to stretch, to rise or raise, to rotate or turn. He also laid down certain rules for balance, on the need to bend the knees always as a preparation for any kind of step followed by a stretch, on the vital use of the head and on the need for the co-ordination of all parts if the desired movements were to be precise and elegant.

John Weaver designated dancers as the Serious, the Grotesque and, most importantly, the Scenical, 'who practise Stage dancing' which was 'to Explain things conceived in the Mind by the Gestures and Motions of the Body and plainly and intelligently representing Actions, Motions and Passions so that the Spectator might perfectly understand the Performer by these his Motions, although he say no Word'. Weaver was the first to create a *ballet d'action* in which the dancers told their own story. His ideas were taken to Paris by Marie Sallé and the Italian Comedians led by Luigi Riccoboni. From there Weaver's ideas spread throughout Europe.

Jean-Georges Noverre in his *Letters on Dance* (1760) described the seven movements which give steps their varying qualities, namely: to bend, stretch, rise, jump, glide, dart and turn. He also described the four types of professional dancer whom he used in his ballets. Noverre distinguished his dancers by their particular physiques and personalities, whereas Weaver had judged them by their ability to act. Most of Noverre's ballets dealt with heroes and heroines from Greek, Roman and other epic sources, all of whom had characteristics in common, as do so many modern heroes and heroines.

Danseurs nobles and ballerinas

These dancers were placed in the first of Noverre's categories. Their dancing was highly dignified and best suited to aristocratic roles or, as he was to say later (1810), 'those of noble birth, the only appropriate heroes and heroines for ballets staged at the Paris Opera'. They had to be well-proportioned, elegant and behave as rulers of a kingdom and thus able to command the attention of all. The tempi of their dances were usually slow and grandiloquent, the gestures generous yet precise and performed with conviction. The heroes and heroines of Petipa's ballets are an example of this category. Today such dancers are rare, but others can assume these roles because technique has advanced.

Danseurs and danseuses classiques

Noverre's second category comprised those dancers whom he expected to be technical perfectionists. They were often shorter and plumper than those of the first category, excelling in *pirouettes*, *élévation* and *batterie*, because of their natural gift of *ballon*. They had livelier personalities and danced roles such as Diana, goddess of the hunt, or Mercury, messenger of the gods. Their dances were usually fast and had to display their exciting footwork, e.g. Petipa's Bluebird. Because of the present-day search for virtuosity many dancers can attempt such roles after they have mastered its technique.

Demi-caractère dancers

Although Noverre did not specifically name them he described these dancers' particular characteristics as having similar physiques and technical expertise as the *danseurs classiques* but they were not always so well-proportioned and usually possessed a natural sense of comedy. They were in demand to play fantastic or comic roles such as satyrs or jesters and were used to relieve the solemnity of late eighteenth- and ninteenth-century ballets, e.g. the many jesters found in Petipa and Soviet ballets and Puck in Ashton's *The Dream*. True *demi-caractère* dancers with a sense of comedy are still rare but they are to be found. They are often most valuable members of a company because of their ability to sink their own personalities in order to play a range of entirely unusual characters such as the comic Alain in *La Fille Mal Gardée*, the tragic Bratfisch in *Mayerling*, Kolia, the son, in *A Month in the Country* and the ridiculous short dancer in *Elite Syncopations*.

Character dancers

Noverre called his fourth group character dancers, that is those whose physique and movements were not necessarily of the finest but whose abilities when playing some comic or dramatic role such as a Cyclops or Fury were most valuable. Such talent is still most valuable to choreographers wishing to bring reality to the stage by contrasting youth and age, naivety and experience, the peasant and the aristocrat. Such actor-dancers play an important, sometimes vital, part whenever convincing mime and characterisation are predominant features in a production.

Examples are Father Thomas in Ashton's *La Fille Mal Gardée* and Bottom in *The Dream*. In addition there are dancers whose forte is to demonstrate the different national styles when Scottish, Polish, Hungarian and other national dances are included in such ballets as *Coppélia* and *Swan Lake*.

These four distinct types of dancer are still found in twentieth-century ballet companies. They are, of course, required for the older works in the repertoire and probably in newer story ballets where all ages should be seen if a plot is to have credibility. They are found in such widely differing ballets as MacMillan's *Romeo and Juliet* and *The Invitation* and as Ashton's *Enigma Variations* and *A Month in the Country*. This is why the same physical types and personalities are still represented amongst the students of professional schools. However, it must be said that true *danseurs nobles* and *classiques* are rare. This is because demands for virtuosity have grown as well as for greater physical flexibility. Choreographers are creating much more complicated and longer *enchaînements*, particularly for their *pas de deux*, and they give their dancers greater freedom to break the strictly conventional rules of class-room technique. Sufficient time is not always given to the study of the basic principles and the proper spacing and placing of the movements. Instead of concentrating on the lines of the dance – which they will need if they ever dance in Ashton's *Symphonic Variations* or *Monotones*, MacMillan's *Requiem* or Bintley's *Consort Lessons* – students spend more time loosening up to meet the demands of modern choreographers. There is often a rush to create something new without enough thought being given to the physical problems they may cause.

There remain, however, a few dancers who excel in the purely classical roles, which an audience demands because they are still testing grounds for particular talents. Purely classical ballets are still popular, so there have to be choreographers who understand and mould the technique. They must know how to make use of and when necessary discard the old conventional rules. They must retain the calm spaciousness of movement if they are not to destroy the essence of the classical style. Balanchine, Ashton, MacMillan and now Bintley break many conventions, but they never lose sight of its true qualities in those of their ballets which can be called classical.

PART 3

BALLET-MAKING

Kinds of ballet

When choreographers have studied all the available sources of inspiration, they should consider what kind of ballet they want to create. There are roughly three kinds all of which can use one or a mixture of dance styles.

The story ballet

A story ballet demands that the circumstances and events occurring as the plot unfolds will be seen to affect the lives and personalities of the characters involved and that dance and gesture will express moods, emotions and action. Since Fokine broke away from the rigid categories of dance or mime, twentieth-century choreographers, following his example, have usually created a continuous design of expressive movement which interprets the story by means of mimed dance or danced mime (see page 58). The stories can range from the most tragic such as *The Rake's Progress*, *Romeo and Juliet* and *Mayerling* to the lyrical fantasy of *The Dream* and from the subtle and poignant *A Month in the Country* to the happily funny *La Fille Mal Gardée* or the rumbustious *Pineapple Poll*. But no matter whether the ballet lasts one, two or three acts the choreographer must be fully in control of his material so that every detail of the characterisation of the whole cast is appropriate to the general atmosphere and environment within which the plot unfolds. This is particularly important in a three-act ballet where any temptation to display dance 'for its own sake' can lead to the introduction of *divertissements* merely to fill in time or show off all the dancers in the company, but is not concerned with the unfolding of the story. Petipa was often accused of doing this, the best example being the dances by characters from other fairy tales who come to Aurora's wedding (*The Sleeping Beauty*). In a short story ballet this intrusion of extra materials is unlikely. Each dance should arise naturally from the context and reveal something about one or another or all the characters in reaction to a series of situations. Particularly valuable examples of the amount of information which can be given about a character in brief solos are those for most of the characters in *A Month in the Country* and, dramatically, for those in *Mayerling*.

Ballets with a theme

The second kind of ballet describes a theme and this often requires the choreographer closely to observe the behaviour and possibly the customs, ways of moving and moods of a particular group of people. They can come from the world of fantasy as in *Les Sylphides* or reality as in *Enigma Variations*. The latter is an unusual work because it is about people who really lived at a particular period and who had particular relationships with each other. No matter whether the theme comes from fantasy or reality every movement should be lightly or firmly drawn into an overall dance design. It must also delineate the personalities and behaviour of the characters. These designs can reveal people at play during a party as in *Les Rendezvous* or on an ice-rink as in *Les Patineurs*; they present the conflicting or subtle moods arising from the tragedy of lost youth and hope during war-time, as in *Gloria*; or they show how deep sorrow gradually changes into resignation and on to exaltation as in *Requiem*. There can be great variety within some themes. For example, Balanchine in his *Four Temperaments* (with music by Hindemith) describes the moods of a melancholic, sanguine, phlegmatic and choleric man or woman. Ashton in *Façade* and MacMillan in *Elite Syncopations* describe how dancing is such fun when influenced by 'show biz' fashions of a particular period by particular kinds of people.

In all the ballets just mentioned not one makes use of the purely classical technique with its severe class-room discipline. Yet this is the firm basis from which the choreographers built their framework of steps, poses and gestures before painting in the personal touches which describe each performer as an individual with a right to speak in a particular way.

Ballets about dance and abstract ballets

When a choreographer wishes to make a statement about dance that is inspired by a piece of music, he has to answer the question as to what style of dance is appropriate.

The answer largely lies in the music chosen, because music is usually, if not always, the source of the inspiration. Dance can be of a fairly severe classical style as in Ashton's *Scènes de Ballet* which reflects Stravinsky's own description of his score: 'This music is patterned after the form of classical dance' (see page 43). Alternatively, dance can be in an entirely modern idiom as in Martha Graham's *Diversions of Angels* (with music by Dello Joio, 1948) one of her most lyrical works. Whichever style is used in plotless ballets the choreographer should submit to the structure of the music, particularly if the score develops according to the classical techniques of composition. Classical dance is by its very nature soundless, whereas much folk, character and theatre dance use the sound of the dancers' feet, hand-clapping, foot-stamping and occasional verbal comment to emphasise the rhythmic beat and phrasing of the dance. Any style of classically inspired dance needs to be reinforced rhythmically by music which helps to create the timing of the steps within the phrases and also suggests varying qualities, moods and sometimes even emotions. As the critic Ernest Newman wrote: 'Music can become dance when it is subjected to repetition, multiplication and abstraction using steps, poses and gestures with pattern and expression to appeal to both the eye and the intellect' (see also page 47).

The framework of a ballet

Having decided on the story, theme or music, choreographers should consider some vital rules of theatre and construct their ballet in the same way that authors and composers work out their books and compositions. In other words, they must take into account another meaning of the word structure (see page 70) in the sense that it is the basic framework for the choreographic design. As already stated, ballets can be roughly divided into the three different kinds usually danced by companies with a classical repertoire. Firstly there are those which tell a comic or tragic story, such as *La Fille Mal Gardée* or *Romeo and Juliet*. Secondly, there are those which describe a theme, such as *Les Patineurs* or *Elite Syncopations*. Thirdly, there are those which can be called abstract ballets, among which are *Symphonic Variations* and *Monotones I and II*.

Although the ballets mentioned are very different in style, quality and content, they have several things in common because they have to be theatrically viable. Firstly, all ballets need a beginning, a climax and an end. Secondly, they should conform to the unities of time, place and action. That is, a particular action (even if it is only dancing) takes place during a particular period and in a particular environment. These two requirements were first established by Greek playwrights and were later codified by the Académie Française (1635) when it laid down rules for the composition of any literary work. The rules are still valid and the libretto of any ballet neglecting them often fails to hold the attention of its audience because the content has been weakened by too many irrelevances.

Enigma Variations   Ashton's interpretation of Elgar's 'My friends pictured within' (The Royal Ballet)

'A play must have a beginning, a climax and an end' (Aristotle)

A choreographer inspired to create any one of the three kinds of ballet described above would be wise to consider Aristotle's dictum.

Every ballet must have a beginning because every ballet begins with a dancer or dancers making an entrance or being discovered on stage. It must establish at once what type of character each is to play in the plot and the relationship of each to the environment of a theme or the style of dance being used. Dancers on stage must establish their relationship to each other and to those who enter and also the particular way they are to set the action or dance going by initiating the phrasing, style and expressiveness of the choreographic design to be unfolded.

The ballet must have a climax. The relationship of dancers to each other usually leads to a climax of some kind, possibly a confrontation or conflict, perhaps an exciting *pas de deux* or a feat of virtuosity. In the case of a ballet interpreting music, strong distinctions can be made between two movements of different tempo.

The ballet must have an end. No matter which kind of ballet is being performed, it must be drawn to a proper conclusion. It can be the outcome of a confrontation or conflict, e.g. *Giselle* and *Romeo and Juliet*. It can be a group picture, e.g. *Enigma Variations*; a solitary figure mourning lost love and youth, e.g. *A Month in the Country* or enjoying himself, e.g. *Les Patineurs*; or, more rarely, the curtain falling on an empty stage, e.g. *Gloria*, possibly the most dramatic ending of all.

Plotting a story ballet: the unities of time, place and action

There are other considerations to be taken into account when the ballet has a story. The same rules apply whether the plot is tragic or comic.

The first part introduces the characters and shows how they set the action going because of their relationship or attitude to each other. This leads to conflict between individuals (*Giselle*) or groups (*Romeo and Juliet*). The conflict develops in the second part where it reaches a climax: in *Giselle* a death, in *Romeo and Juliet* several deaths. The third part describes the outcome of the conflict and the fate of the protagonists.

Some examples of how to plot

When Bournonville discussed the construction of a ballet he referred to the librettos and development of plot in *La Sylphide* and *Giselle*. He considered both were good examples for others to follow and deplored the long Petipa ballets which lost their meaning through the inclusion of innumerable *divertissements* in which: 'Petipa only devised new difficulties for the dancers.'

Although *La Sylphide* and *Giselle* are two-act ballets with one change of scene, both Taglioni and Perrot (the latter with the help of the writer, Saint-Georges) divided the ballets into three distinct parts.

1 In the first part the leading characters are introduced in their proper setting before a meeting takes place. In *La Sylphide*, James is seen dreaming in his farmhouse before *La Sylphide* awakens and dances with him. Later, apparently unseen by others, she dances through the betrothal party at which he is confronted by Madge, the Witch, who foretells that he will never marry. He throws Madge from the room. In *Giselle* Albrecht enters, in peasant clothes, and knocks on Giselle's cottage door. After persuading her to dance with him, he swears to marry her. The entrance of a hunting party leads to Giselle's meeting with Bathilde, a crucial moment in the plot.

2 The second part of both ballets can be called the climax. James follows *La Sylphide* into the woods, unable to resist her charms, while Madge and her coven are seen stirring a magic brew into which they dip a silken scarf. Giselle discovers Albrecht's deceit when Bathilde confronts her with the fact that the Count Albrecht is her fiancé. This leads to Giselle's madness and death.

3 The third scene in both ballets shows what ensues from these climaxes. James captures *La Sylphide* with the magic scarf. She loses her wings and dies, leaving him to be cursed by Madge. In the latter, Albrecht comes to pray at Giselle's grave. When the Queen of the Wilis commands Giselle to rise and dance him to his death, so strong is her love that she helps him to dance until cockcrow when he will survive. As dawn breaks, she returns to her grave leaving him to mourn alone.

Most other story ballets can be analysed in much the same way. Those with a theme, or which consist of dance only, have a similar plan. A choreographer who neglects the old rules and any item pertinent to the unfolding of the plot, theme or music is demanding a great deal from an audience. Many plotless or so-called abstract ballets, by choreographers such as Balanchine, have no specific characters or climaxes but they do follow the composer's score very closely. Most composers of specially commissioned music, even those later than Stravinsky, follow the time-honoured rules of thematic continuity and development and above all rhythmic phrasing. Good phrasing is all important: it has to set and keep the dancers going. Balanchine would have been the last person to break or contradict the thematic content and destroy the composer's intentions.

The layout of a story ballet

The layout of a story ballet or *ballet d'action* was first conceived by John Weaver in 1717 when he did away with actors and/or singers to tell the story. In his *The Loves of Mars and Venus* the dancers had to tell their own story in different ways. Four main kinds of action were later named by French balletmasters as:

Scènes d'action during which some part of the story was told in conventional gesture, e.g. the casting of Carabosse's spell and the Lilac Fairy's response in the first scene of *The Sleeping Beauty*.

Pas d'action such as solos or *pas de deux* in which dancers portray the character each represents by depicting mood, emotion and action, e.g. again in *The Sleeping Beauty*, the Four Princes express their admiration for Aurora and she returns their compliments in the Rose Adage.

Variations which display the solo dancing ability of each character and define social status and other traits that are so important to the unfolding of the story, e.g. the Six Fairies bring their various gifts to the Christening and Aurora dances happily to acknowledge the compliments of the Princes and all who have come to her birthday (*The Sleeping Beauty*).

Divertissements which were and still are a display of dances that may or may not be applicable to the plot. These dances mattered very much to Petipa and all nineteenth-century balletmasters because they were expected to show off the wealth of talent found in the many Imperial, Royal and State theatres, e.g. all the characters from other fairy tales who came to Aurora's wedding and the character dances in *Swan Lake*.

Mimed dance and danced mime

However, the strict division of a ballet into four distinct kinds was eliminated by Fokine when he totally cut the *scène d'action* from his first ballets and never replaced them. Instead, he used what he called mimed dance or danced mime, insisting, when asked for an explanation, that there was a subtle difference between them, 'only one of degree'.

To Fokine, *Les Sylphides* was mimed dance because he had incorporated a few conventional gestures into his choreography. Fokine said that every 'phrase of his dance was a gesture', and explained: 'Undoubtedly an *arabesque* has many meanings but only when it appears as an idealised gesture. It is a very apparent gesture (in *Les Sylphides*), a yearning for height, for distance, an inclination of the whole body, a movement of the entire being. If there is not this feeling, if it is only a raising of the leg, the *arabesque* becomes intolerable nonsense.' Would-be choreographers should study how Ashton uses this gesture, whether he is telling a story, describing a theme or conveying the feel of the music. They may then realise the truth of Fokine's words.

Petrushka   Foline's second Russian ballet
The Puppets dance in the market place (The Royal Ballet)

On the other hand, Fokine insisted that most of *Petrushka* was danced mime, explaining that the dances performed in the fairground were the only real ones: 'These were not my own work as such crowds would have danced like that any way. But even if the movements made by the three Puppets inside their rooms might seem like dance to some – those who perform them must be actors who can dance.'

Since Fokine showed that dancers must also be able to act if they are to live out the story or theme, very few choreographers have used the almost static *scènes d'action* which stop the flow of dance. Yet, and very often, even a single emphatic conventional gesture performed in a moment of stillness can be tremendously effective and make a strong point in what may otherwise be a continuous flow of dance. Some of the best examples of the single gesture of great significance are to be found in Ashton's *A Month in the Country* and MacMillan's *The Invitation*.

Descriptive and narrative dance

Mimed dance or danced mime can also be called descriptive or narrative dance. Descriptive dance applies to those passages, which can be communicated by dance, which portray everything about a role working within a story or theme, i.e. type of character, period, location, etc. Narrative dance applies to those phrases of conversation between individuals or between dancers and public, where the dancer uses explicit gestures. These ideas are no better illustrated than by Massine in his *The Three-Cornered Hat*. The success of these two means of communication is largely due to the nature of De Falla's score, which is somewhat like that of Stravinsky for *The Firebird* and *Petrushka*. De Falla borrowed elements from Spanish folk song and dance for all the descriptive passages. Narrative dance is used in the conversations between the Miller, his Wife and their canary, and between the Wife and the Corregidor, which are based on flamenco music. This is usually performed extempore, following the whims of the singer, musician and/or dancer. It is therefore slightly erratic in phrase, rhythm and tune. Such irregularity makes these conversations appear spontaneous, an element which Massine was careful to preserve. Thus there are no repetitions of sentences. To a very large extent this is what Ashton does in *A Month in the Country* where the non-dancers speak out from time to time in explicit gestures. Most of MacMillan's ballets, particularly *Mayerling*, contain the same juxtaposition of descriptive and narrative. This is of extreme value and should be used more often by young choreographers.

Continuity and the use of the leitmotif

Once the basic structure for a story ballet has been created, the choreographer must find ways of linking the beginning, climax and end so that the plot develops easily from one scene to the next. This can be effected by the use of a leitmotif or phrases of music.

Since the first performance of *Giselle*, certain composers and arrangers have used leitmotifs for one or several characters and repeat the leitmotifs each time the characters appear. These musical phrases give continuity to the action and are most valuable because they help both performers and audience to understand how moments in the story or theme affect the players. Adolphe Adam, composer of the music for *Giselle*, initiated this idea which greatly influenced Wagner and later composers.

Leitmotifs are a firm point of reference that carries the dancer onwards from the

Giselle   The Old Romantic ballet – Perrot's leitmotifs
Above: Giselle counts the petals; below: Giselle throws the flowers to Albrecht (Ravenna Tucker, Jay Jolley; Ravenna Tucker)

beginning to the climax and to the end of the story. Adam provided Giselle with five leitmotifs which Perrot (the choreographer of her dances) matched with five brief *enchaînements*. These change slightly with the music as the plot unfolds and allow Giselle to develop from a simple peasant dancer in love with Albrecht to a tragically distraught maiden and finally to the ethereal Wili. The leitmotifs for Giselle created by Adam and Perrot can be said to disclose her emotional development. Prokofiev used several leitmotifs in the same way in his score for *Romeo and Juliet* where they heighten not only the emotional involvement of the hero and heroine but also the conflict between the warring Montagues and Capulets (see page 26).

Although Tchaikovsky used leitmotifs to weave magic threads through his ballets, his have a slightly different purpose. He composed 'The Flight of the Swans' (his own title) to herald each arrival of Odette and the Swans. It was not intended as music for dancing. He similarly composed two leitmotifs to run through *The Sleeping Beauty*. The Lilac Fairy's music is always heard just before and during all her entrances. It is in contrast to another leitmotif that marks the entrances of Carabosse, the wicked fairy. The two tunes underline the conflict between good and evil. Whereas Adam and Prokofiev's leitmotifs heighten the emotional content of the love theme, Tchaikovsky's are there to create the right atmosphere and to emphasise the conflict.

When Stravinsky composed *The Firebird* he used leitmotifs in yet another way. He created very distinctive passages of ascending chords to accompany the magic bird's flight through the trees. They accompany her every entrance. In contrast, he provided passages of descending chords for Kostchei. These two themes illustrate the conflict between life and death, love and hate, youth and age – all three topics being an essential part of any Russian fairy tale. In addition to the two leitmotifs, Stravinsky used traditional songs and dances backed by a mysterious rhythmic sound which helps to heighten the tension. It can be said to be the wind rustling through the trees, when first heard as the Tsarevich climbs over the wall to find his Princess. It keeps the tension going until the Tsarevich breaks the egg and thus signifies the death of Kostchei. Whereupon the music solemnly changes to the traditional Easter hymn of rejoicing, 'At the Gate', as the Tsarevich and his Bride are crowned king and queen.

Stravinsky used similar ideas in his score for *Petrushka* and again provided an underlying rhythmic pulse to represent the incessant throb of the engines in the fairground and the general noise of the excited crowd. The throb occasionally rises above all other sounds and helps to make Petrushka's Cry (Stravinsky's original title) so poignant. When Petrushka is left alone in his room, his cries dominate the stage both musically and choreographically because the incessant throb is not heard. So when the cry is heard again just before the curtain falls it comes as a final appeal for help. There is always a moment of silence before the audience respond, so strong has been the tension.

Prokofiev threaded two leitmotifs through his score for *Cinderella* to mark the heroine and her Fairy Godmother. When Ashton staged his version of the ballet he made Cinderella's leitmotif into a major factor for the development of the plot by creating a matching dance leitmotif. It is first heard and seen when the dancing-master gives the Ugly Sisters a lesson. After they have gone to the ball, Cinderella, with a giggle, picks up her broom and gives it the same lesson, using it as a partner. This introduces several movements seen later in more solemn form when she dances with the Prince at the ball. Some of the same movements are repeated yet again in the final *pas de deux*, when the Prince raises her high above the glistening Stars before leading her away to the land where 'they lived happily ever after', where all fairy tales should end.

Dance leitmotifs can be found in most of Ashton's ballets and are sometimes marked by his particular use of one step or pose. This was first apparent in *The Quest* (1943) where the *arabesques* danced in many ways became the movement through which Una (danced by Margot Fonteyn) expressed the emotions aroused when she is assailed by the Four False Knights and then her joy when rescued by St. George.

Ashton has other ways of creating a leitmotif to link incidents pertinent to the plot throughout a ballet. These are not necessarily created through dance and music. Quite the most enchanting is the leitmotif of pink ribbons being continually tied and untied until Lise and Colas are finally wed in *La Fille Mal Gardée*. The ribbons are first seen when Lise ties them to a nail on the wall. Colas sees them there and ties them to his own crook. Lise retrieves them to tie his hands together. This marks their first exchange of vows, which is reiterated when Lise pretends to harness Colas by the ribbons to a trap of which she is the driver. But not for long, for they make another pledge by tying themselves together in a cat's cradle. Ribbons appear again and again, ultimately in the maypole dance, before they disappear in a flutter of rose petals when Mother Simone relents and blesses the happy couple. There is another leitmotif in this funny, happy ballet, the precious red umbrella, Alain's only love – or so it would seem – for it is the one thing he clings to and simply has to find when he has lost Lise.

The choreographer's viewpoint

Generally speaking, choreographers can approach their task in three different ways.

An objective view

Choreographers wish to express themselves through dance because a story, theme or music has inspired them. Their work will require strict adherence by the dancers to a distinctive style of dance and gesture, which is designed to communicate thoughts, moods, emotions and actions as the plot, theme or dance unfolds. They insist that there must be no deviation from that style and demand such loyalty that their dancers lose their own identity and become absorbed in the world of that particular ballet. Fokine was the first choreographer to distinguish the need for a particular style for each ballet when he created such different ballets as *Les Sylphides*, *Le Carnaval*, *Prince Igor*, *The Firebird* and *Petrushka*. From his innovations have come many developments opening the way for similar independently minded choreographers. They also opened the eyes of the audience to the endless possibilities of expressing meaning through dance. Three particularly objective masters of choreography are de Valois in *Job* and *The Rake's Progress*, Massine with such different ballets as *The Good-Humoured Ladies* and *The Three-Cornered Hat* and MacMillan with *Mayerling* and *Requiem*.

A subjective view

Choreographers can also take a more subjective view of their work. This is equally important and has so proved throughout ballet history. The choreographer seizes on the personality of a particular dancer and creates ballets through which the dancer gradually develops and discloses unique talent and qualities to such a degree that audiences soon recognise a star. The names of four choreographers immediately stand

The Firebird   Fokine's first national ballet
Above: the Firebird sings her lullaby; below: the Coronation 'At the Gate' (Antoinette Sibley; Deanne Bergsma, Anthony Dowell and The Royal Ballet)

La Fille Mal Gardée   Ashton's English comic masterpiece
Above: Lise and Colas are drawn together by the pink ribbons; below: Alain misses Lise's kiss (Wendy
Ellis, Wayne Eagling, Guy Niblett and The Royal Ballet)

out. Taglioni recognised his daughter Marie's quality of other worldliness in *La Sylphide*; Perrot discovered Carlotta Grisi's unique qualities as an actress-dancer in *Giselle*; Fokine exposed Tamara Karsavina's many-sided brilliance in such works as *The Firebird*, *Le Carnaval* and *Petrushka*; Ashton fostered Margot Fonteyn's varied personality.

A fifth choreographer must be added to this list. Kenneth MacMillan is a master of many styles and views but it was he who first revealed Lynn Seymour's dramatic gifts in *Romeo and Juliet* and has more recently been doing the same for Darcey Bussell. Perhaps because he is in many ways an absolutely objective choreographer, he successfully exposes his deeply held views on society and its problems, in particular man's inhumanity to man, through dance. His two profoundly moving ballets, *Gloria* and *Requiem*, the one a poem for lost youth and hope through the onset of war and the other a song of mourning and praise for a departed friend, stand and fall by the audience's response to their message and not to the pre-eminence of a star.

Would the ballerinas named above have reached the same eminence without the personal attention of a choreographer of genius? It does not really matter what the answer is. A choreographer's wish to exploit a particularly gifted dancer usually leads that dancer to develop more fully and to have more to give when cast in ballets by more objective choreographers. In such cases, the dancer has to submit to the discipline of style and context dictated and not created for them. This experience generally makes them more versatile artists. No better example can be given than by citing the careers of Tamara Karsavina and Margot Fonteyn, both of whom worked with many different choreographers as well as submitting themselves to the severely classical discipline of the older Petipa repertoire.

A general view

There is a third type of choreographer who produces ballets which give audiences great pleasure through the sheer variety of their virtuoso designs. Because of the interesting, usually technical, demands made on the performers, their ballets often become testing grounds for future soloists. Variations from such ballets as Petipa's *Don Quixote*, *Raymonda* and *La Bayadère* and Bournonville's *Napoli* are still considered by most classical dancers to be more technically demanding than the more complex twistings and turnings of modern choreographers who mix their styles. This is because a lack of technical expertise in a Petipa variation danced in a 'tutu' is all too obvious, whilst its lack in modern works usually goes unnoticed. In classical technique, the calm spaciousness and perfection of each part of an *enchaînement* flows onwards in line as part of whole sentences in the choreographic design.

The contents of a choreographic vocabulary

Dance is a language which contains verbs (or steps) that give continuity and lead up to, through and from the nouns to create a design in movement. The nouns are the poses or gestures which, with the semi-colons, commas, colons and full stops, give expression. The choreographer must understand how to form sentences or *enchaînements* which will make sense in the context of the ballet. Because the verbs (steps) are the vital links in any *enchaînement* they must be performed in a manner suitable to the context and the music. To do so, both verbs and nouns need to be qualified by adjectives and/or adverbs determined by the choreographers during the making of the design. Firstly, they can give them physical shape by referring to Noverre's seven movements of dance, viz. to bend, stretch, rise, jump, glide, dart and turn. Secondly, they should decide in what manner and why they are so performed to give appropriate expression and sustain a style throughout the whole design.

Choreographers today also need to understand what can be called a Grammar of Choreography if their work is to emerge as a valid stage presentation. They can no longer concern themselves only with the technical aspect of class-room steps and poses. There are, therefore, other items that should be included in the contents of such a Grammar. Useful definitions are given by the *Oxford English Dictionary*.

Grammar

'The art or science dealing with a language's inflexions and other means of showing the relation between words'

This definition raises many questions for the choreographer. Dance movement in every form and style must be correctly parsed and expressed if it is to be clearly understood whether its message is simple, subtle, bold, comic or tragic. Movement makes its proper effect when the choreographer has selected and co-ordinated appropriate movements to make sentences flow from one to another with such style, quality and expression that the design makes sense. This can be achieved only if there is motive.

Motive

'Tending to initiate; that which induces a person to act'

Every choreographer must have a motive if he or she is to give proper thought, impetus and significance to the movements made by the dancers whether: they are telling a story; describing and/or expressing the thoughts behind a theme; or interpreting music either by expressing personal feelings about the melody and rhythm or by so framing the dance that it parallels the music and reveals its structure.

In all three types of work choreographers must give the dancers reasons for their movements. To do this they will need not only a knowledge of the vocabulary of steps through which dancers communicate, but an ability to explain their design so that dancers can give it depth of feeling (see page 78).

Motion

'Manner of moving the body as in walking, running, dancing, etc.'

If choreographers are to justify their reasons for creating a ballet, they should use or create a style of movement appropriate to and expressive of the characters in the story being told and their moods, emotions and actions. The dancers or players in a theme ballet will need to convey the general atmosphere and any other element pertinent to the situation in which they find themselves, as well as the mood and content of the music chosen to give them phrasing. They will need to do the same if they are interpreting music.

Today there are many ballets which are created in the generally accepted styles from which choreographers can borrow: classical, *demi-caractère*, romantic, character and/or national, and modern (see pages 75-138). However, when necessary, choreographers can and should create a particular style that is perhaps based on a mixture of the above but that is, in the final analysis, a style suitable for one ballet only. Such choreographers as Ashton, MacMillan and Robbins have produced some ballets which have an exclusive style of their own. The most outstanding are possibly *Monotones*, *Gloria* and *Afternoon of a Faun*. Although the movements in all three are classically based, they would look out of place in older classical ballets or danced to other music.

Impetus

'Force with which a body moves; the impetus to move in dance; impulse to create'

For the purpose of a choreographic grammar the word 'impetus' can be interpreted in three ways all of which are applicable to the design.

The first meaning should be understood as the inspiration which has urged the choreographer to create. The sources of inspiration are seemingly endless (see page 17). Many enduring ballets have been inspired by stories from world literature. Others describe a pastime such as skating, concert-going and even a dance party. Other choreographers find disturbing themes of madness, the tragedy of war and man's inhumanity to man. There have even been attempts to stage biographies, one of the first being Loring's *Billy the Kid* (see page 30). Choreographers who are inspired to interpret music can do so in many ways, all of which can be successful, but only if they remember that its overall rhythm is not merely a mechanical guide to the timing of the steps within the dance design (see page 68).

The second meaning of the word 'impetus' should be applied to the actual performance of any step or pose in the purely technical sense. That is, the choreographer must understand from which part of the body impetus is to be given so that the step achieves its full purpose at the proper moment – usually in some gesture and its musical emphasis. The moment can be as the dancer pauses momentarily in a pose, as a comma in the middle or as a full stop at the end of a sentence. Or the moment can be an important point in an overall design to fill space, such as the moment in a *grand jeté en avant* when the dancer's two legs are at an equal height from the ground and he or she appears to travel onwards effortlessly through space. It can also be the moment when a dancer moves into a *pirouette* and spins before holding a pose.

However, more important is the third meaning of impetus which has also to do with physical performance. Impetus is again needed, particularly in a story ballet, when it has to be given to emphasise the significance of a step. This always used to happen in older ballets when the hero would take a step forward with a slight stamp before he 'swore to marry' the heroine.

Impetus given from or with any part of the body must coincide with the musical phrasing for it indicates the performer is to make or is making an important statement. Even in softly flowing ballets such as *Monotone II* where no impetus should be seen as deliberate, it must nevertheless be there and firmly controlled if, for example, the two boys are to turn the girl *sur pointe* with her working leg stretched upwards and her head and body bent downwards over her supporting leg.

Sometimes it is valuable to emphasise the impetus itself, particularly if a bravura *pirouette* is needed to display a dancer's particular expertise or perhaps some exhibitionist trait in the character portrayed. This can be most effective in cases where the dancer takes a slow preparation into a firm but slight *demi-plié* then suddenly rises and turns five or six times. This kind of bravura performance is only legitimate if the context and music allow the dancer to 'steal a little time'. Most classical choreographers still use this device when working with nineteenth-century ballet music, which was often written to order by a composer understanding the choreographer's desire to show off a dancer. Since the days of Diaghilev and his commissioning of scores exclusive to one ballet from such composers as Stravinsky, this pandering to technical prowess has rarely happened. The impetus for any step, pose or gesture should be part of the overall rhythm of the ballet.

Rhythm

'Metrical movement determined by the various relations of long and short, or accented and unaccented beats', e.g. the choreographer's arrangement of steps and poses

The above definition does not adequately answer the question: 'What is rhythm?' if the choreographer is to understand how the uses of rhythm must be applied to the creation of a ballet. The late Frank Howes showed an understanding of the problems facing a choreographer when he wrote: 'Every dance has its own rhythm, just as every dancer has an inborn sense of measuring time because each movement must be felt to flow through the whole body as well as the space in which it moves. Without a sense of rhythm our sense of time is devoid of landmarks. It is the particular organisation of movement in time, space and intensity that a choreographer achieves through his grouping of the various types of steps. He can create overall rhythms and within them short phrase rhythms, but the basis of them all is that they exist in groups and by being efficient in action and appropriate to the context give pleasure to both the performer and the onlooker.' (See also page 41.)

Rhythm in ballet is not therefore a mere time-keeper as it is in such social ballroom dances as waltzes and fox-trots. A ballet for the stage must have an overall rhythm which sets the atmosphere, quality, mood and possibly the emotional content of the whole. And ballet must also have short phrase rhythms which will give it variety, dimension, mass, structure, texture and style.

Perhaps no ballet has ever made the same impact on dancers and audience as Stravinsky's *Rite of Spring*. Its urgent overall rhythm commands the choreographer to keep the dancers moving forever onwards with greater intensity to the climax, whilst the shorter phrase rhythms give the Chosen Maiden and smaller groups such ways of moving that they hold the audience's full attention until the fall of the curtain.

Variety

'Being various; absence of monotony or uniformity; class of things differing in some common qualities from the rest of a larger class to which they belong'

The important point in the above definition is the assertion that things which differ in some common qualities do nevertheless belong to the larger class. In other words, the choreographer should set out to create a particular style for the whole dance design, yet within it be free to vary the way of performing a step without breaking away from or distorting the overall rhythmic quality and phrasing of his *enchaînements*.

It does not matter on which style of dance a choreographer bases his design. It should be obvious that there are many ways of performing any step, pose or gesture.

The usual ways can be seen in any class-room and are based on the four movements dictated by the natural anatomical structure of the body, namely: to bend (contract), stretch (relax), rise (raise), turn (rotate). These can take place anywhere by the correct use of the bones, joints, tendons, ligaments and muscles. The ways in which these four actions can be co-ordinated are extremely varied. Altering the look of a step can involve changing the time signature or tempo to which it is danced, the direction it takes or a change of *épaulement*, its quality and expressiveness, to name but a few. The choreographer's problem is to select which of the movements are appropriate, when and how they are to be incorporated and what style and quality they require.

Dimension

'Measurable extent of any kind; number of unknown qualities contained as factors in a whole'

Dimension immediately suggests that the choreographer must take into account the space in which the dancers move. Although this is of considerable importance, particularly if the ballet is to be presented in a large theatre, too much concentration on certain of the dimensions (height, depth or breadth) may deprive some members of the audience of much of the pattern. For example, too much weaving and rolling of bodies on the floor is hardly visible from the stalls, whilst too much concentration on one side of the stage finds spectators on the same side craning their necks to see what is going on. It was for such reason that most of Petipa's famous *pas de deux* take place centre stage, whilst those of Ashton and MacMillan cover the whole area as befits their more flowing lyrical styles.

Dimension does not merely mean the space to be filled. It must also refer to the depth of thought behind the design whether the subject deals with a bold tale or a subtle philosophical, psychological or even theological theme. It may even present a comic, frivolous or bawdy joke to arouse laughter or attempt to reveal the workings of a composer's mind. However, choreographers should always remember that whatever story, theme or music is chosen, it must be translated into clear, often simple, dance statements understandable by an audience. It should not be necessary to compile long programme notes, except perhaps in those cases where a poem is being interpreted (see page 28). Choreographers should never assume that all in the audience have sufficient knowledge of the subject, theme and ideas which are possibly understood only by an exclusive coterie of friends. This does not mean that only well-known or straightforward subjects and themes are to be staged. Far from it. Shakespeare's dramas of *Hamlet*, *Romeo and Juliet* and *Othello* have many subtle touches of humour and tenderness, as do his lighter works such as *A Midsummer Night's Dream*. All have been translated into successful choreographic form. Similarly the delicate and subtle nuances of such ballets as Ashton's *A Month in the Country*, Robbins' *Dances at a Gathering* and MacMillan's *Song of the Earth* are successfully conveyed and capture the audience's attention from the moment the curtain rises by the impetus, rhythm, dimension and variety of dance. Dance in all its aspects has proved capable of embracing the whole range of emotions and behaviour that emerge from a proper reading and understanding of the text.

Mass

'Coherent body of matter of indefinite shape or dense aggregation of objects, or assembly of people'

The above definition may at first seem to have little to do with a choreographer's work. But if the choreographer does not understand all the details which go to make the total presentation of a ballet, it can all too easily fail in some way or other. Merely to count all the details that it is necessary to accumulate from the preparation of a scenario and score through rehearsal to public performance should make it clear that co-operation from other artists as well as from dancers is required. There must be a librettist – if the choreographer does not plan out the plot – a composer or arranger of music, a designer for set and costumes and all those associated with sets and props, painting, stage-managing, lighting and everything else needed to 'get the curtain up'.

An understanding of 'mass' in choreographic terms only means how to organise and manipulate the dancers within that mass of objects. Are they to take pride of place, as they should in ballets worthy of the name? Or is dance going to be overloaded and the choreographic design lost in a mass of stage materials, such as too-heavy costumes, an overdose of stage effects and machinery or over-powerful sets which dwarf the dancers. These are but a few of the hazards that can wreck the look and expression of the choreographic design.

An even more important sense of the term 'mass' applies to the choreographer's handling of his cast. Is it small or large and who is to play a general or particular part in the action? Can certain individuals be directed in such a way that they stand out from the mass because they are the tellers of the story, the chief exponents in the drama or theme? Or do they play only a minor role which nevertheless gives a vital clue to the unfolding of the plot? Or must they remain part of the 'mass', in other words the *corps de ballet*, because they are needed to create the proper atmosphere, state the location, suggest the mood and very often respond to whatever is taking place? To do this successfully the choreographer must be able to select from the 'aggregation of objects' only those which are appropriate to the ballet in hand.

Structure

'Manner in which a building or other complete whole is constructed; supporting framework'

This definition is to be construed as the way in which the choreographer designs the layout of the ballet. It is particularly appropriate in the case of a ballet that tells a story where the libretto has to be set out in such a way that the action can be logically developed and each item roughly timed. Such a libretto can then be handed to a composer or arranger of music and a designer so that they can make their contributions to the total production. At first the libretto is only an outline of how the story unfolds and what part each member of the cast is supposed to play. It also needs a brief explanation of how and why they make their entrances and exits. The following questions arise, although not necessarily in this order.

1 Is the tale to be told in the short space of thirty or forty minutes with a minimal cast? If so, then care should be taken to dispense with any dancer or item not essential to the action, e.g. Ashton eliminated several characters in Turgenev's *A Month in the Country*. Or is it to be a full-length ballet with a maximum use of dancers? However long or short the work, care is needed not to overload the tale with *variations* and *divertissements*. It should only include items which increase tension as in *Romeo and Juliet* or give rise to more fun and happiness as in *La Fille*

Mal Gardée, or enhance the general mood as in *A Month in the Country* where there is romance in the air and also a general feeling of frustration. Moreover no matter the size of part each dancer has to play in the unfolding of the plot or the quality of each dancer's place in the dance design, everything must be mapped in every aspect.

2 How is the story to be unfolded? Is use to be made of the strictly ordered old-fashioned *scènes* and *pas d'action*, *variations* and/or *divertissements*? Or is it to be told by mimed dance and/or danced mime? The latter methods are used by every modern choreographer working with classical dance because it is more flexible and expressive and many dancers trained in its technique are capable of acting out the deepest emotions of the characters played, as Ashton and MacMillan have continually shown. Yet even mimed dance and danced mime need to be carefully structured if the story is to be told in all its aspects. There are *scènes d'action* in *Romeo and Juliet*: for example, when Lord and Lady Capulet bring Paris to confront Juliet in her bedroom which merges into a *pas d'action* as she repulses his advances when he tries to woo her; there is the variation describing the activities of Romeo, Mercutio and Benvolio before they enter the ballroom. A similar description can be given to various parts of *A Month in the Country*, such as the *scène d'action* where the entire cast tries to find the lost key, the exquisite *pas d'action* of Vera and the Tutor, and Kolia's excited variation playing with a ball.

3 Once an outline of the story and a general layout of the plot have been decided, they should be discussed with the composer or arranger of music whose first task may be to create a proper beginning with the overture. Is it to set the general atmosphere and mood as Stravinsky did for *The Firebird*? Mysterious sounds of the wind whispering in the trees, the soaring flight of a bird and the heavy tread of an unseen foot are still a wonderful introduction to this magic tale. On the other hand, Prokofiev used his overture to *Romeo and Juliet* to introduce the leitmotifs which will help both dancers and audience to follow the unfolding of the plot. He contrasts the love themes of Romeo and Juliet with those which accompany the bitter struggles and fights between Montague and Capulet. Differently again, the overture to *A Month in the Country* conveys romantic nostalgia with deeper hints of passion which Lanchbery created when he arranged little-known music by Chopin. This music also firmly sets the location and period of the tale.

4 The choreographer's next task is to establish the relationship between two or more players and set the action going. Is the opening to generate atmosphere and mood, to establish the location, time of day and/or period which will give an air of reality? This is the most valuable way of working out a first scene and happens in *Romeo and Juliet*. Here is a market place in a certain town, in a certain period, with the inhabitants setting about their daily tasks as the sun rises. Despite the general activities there is menace in the air and it is not long before the rival factions of Montagues and Capulets are fighting and deaths occurring before the lovers even meet. This opening is very different from the quietly charming first scene of *A Month in the Country*, where the only thing amiss is Natalia's bored behaviour.

Even with such examples in mind the choreographer may well decide it is better to delay the confrontation between the chief players because, by creating and stressing the general atmosphere, this raises the audience's expectations before the meeting of the protagonists, and the sudden onset of passion is what makes the ultimate tragedy so poignant. This happens in *Giselle* where Hilarion's suspicions of Albrecht's identity are already aroused before Albrecht meets Giselle. Hilarion's discovery of Albrecht's sword and later his confrontation with Giselle, with the sword in his hands, still does not convince Giselle of Albrecht's duplicity. It is only later when Bathilde confronts her with the news that Albrecht is her fiancé that Giselle realises the truth and loses her reason.

The scenes between Hilarion, Giselle, Albrecht and Bathilde are reminiscent of the scenes that develop Tybalt's hatred of Romeo from the first fight between Montague and Capulet to his discovery of Romeo with Juliet after their first meeting at the ball, and finally to the fight that ends in Tybalt's death. These scenes heighten the tension and suggest that all will end in tragedy.

Despite the great differences in style between the above three ballets and despite their different libretti the three choreographers Perrot (with Saint-Georges), MacMillan and Ashton give valid reasons why the tragic deaths of Giselle, Romeo and Juliet, and Natalia's lost love are the inevitable result of what has gone before. In other words, what happens at the beginning of the story states why the relationships between two or more characters lead to confrontations which continue onwards to a climax and finally draw the ballet to a suitable conclusion. This last task is possibly the most difficult because the audience must be convinced that the ending chosen is the only possible outcome of everything that has gone before.

The ending can also owe a great deal to the composer or arranger of music. Stravinsky ensures a happy yet solemn ending to *The Firebird* by using the old Easter hymn 'At the Gate' where the whole congregation rejoices at the renewal of life. Lanchbery uses Chopin's poignant *Andante Spinato* to express Natalia's realisation that love has now escaped her. Prokofiev's solemn and doom-laden funeral march finally stamps the tragedy of *Romeo and Juliet* because it has already echoed through each stage in the unfolding of the plot. It seems the inevitable and only way to conclude such a passionate story of love and hate.

5 Similar considerations have to be given to ballets on a theme and to ballets that interpret music where the composer's own structure should inspire the design (see page 41).

Texture
'Arrangement of threads; the characteristic feel or look of this arrangement'

This definition should be understood as the choreographer's ability to establish a style of movement through which the audience will feel and understand what the performers are communicating through a particular way of dancing. The style must disclose and be expressive of the moods, emotions and actions of the roles played even where few personal feelings are allowed to show, as in such ballets as Ashton's *Monotones* where all that is needed is a calm, unhurried and seemingly endless weaving of the dance design in all its dimensions. Nevertheless the three dancers in *Monotones* are expressing their close relationship to each other and to the space in which they dance and above all to the flowing lines of the design and of the musical phrases. The composer Satie confessed to his friends that his music was probably inspired by a study of the friezes on ancient Greek vases. It is surely not surprising that

Ashton was similarly inspired. He selected the simplest steps and poses of classical dance with its perfectly balanced form and at the same time gave it straighter, longer lines to draw attention to the more athletic qualities of Greek dance and to the clear, austere sounds of Satie's modern music. In other words, Ashton created a special style for a ballet with its roots in ancient classical art yet entirely modern in outlook (see page 130).

Choreographers can derive a particular style from any of the usual forms of dance studied in the established schools of France, Russia, Denmark, Italy, England and America. Each school has its own method dictated by the dancers' response to the way that technique is practised, a way which is coloured by national traits in music, society and culture. All dance is based on the same principles and rules which are dictated by the anatomical capacity for movement found in the human body. There are some five main styles to consider: the purely classical, *demi-caractère*, romantic, character and/or national, and modern in its various forms. But before describing these categories it is valuable to consider the meaning of style.

Style

'The artistic expression or way of presenting characteristics proper to the period and/or the subject chosen'

This definition 'proper to the period' is nowhere better exemplified than in Ashton's five classical ballets. In these he has tried to reflect not only the period in which their music was written but also to devise a particular way of dancing inspired by the structure and tone of the particular piece of music (see page 41).

The choreographer must decide what kind of subject has been chosen. For example: is the subject taken from classical literature with its firm structural rules like those which govern Balanchine's *Apollo*? Or is it from romantic poetry or music, such as the Massine-Berlioz *Symphonie Fantastique* or Balanchine's *Double Concerto* based on music by Bach? Or does it re-create a folk tale such as the Fokine-Stravinsky *The Firebird* or a national epic such as Bintley's *The Swan of Tuonela*? Choreographers should then go on to decide which style of dance would be most appropriate. Generally speaking, there are certain well-recognised ways of dancing which can serve as a basis. But more often than not these will all need some adjustment and/or extra touches to make the dance design suitable or, even better, unique for a particular ballet. These touches will depend firstly on the type of character to be portrayed; secondly on how their movements will be affected by the unfolding of the plot, theme and/or music; thirdly on what particular steps, poses and gestures within the total design will be needed to communicate meaning.

Rhapsodie   Ashton's interpretation of Rachmaninov's belief that 'music is movement' (Lesley Collier, Anthony Dowell)

PART 4

STYLES IN BALLET

The classical ballet

The classical style with its particular look and feeling was first described by Pythagoras (5th century BC): 'It represents the subtle equilibrium of outline and axis, by the perfection of its symmetry of balance within a composition.'

De Valois reiterated that thought when she said in a lecture to teachers (1947): 'Classical dance requires an ordered, balanced form in which a calm spaciousness of movement animates the dancers. Any expression it may show arises solely through the inspired personality of a dancer who has mastered its technique.'

A classical ballet has a style of dance based on certain accepted principles and rules laid down by French, Russian, Danish, Italian and more recent schools. Its movements are harmonious, perfectly balanced and symmetrical in design. It follows the restrained style associated with classical antiquity. If it has a story or theme the behaviour and actions of the characters are predictable and conform to the old code of courtly behaviour. Nineteenth-century choreographers who adopted this style defined the characters by certain known habits and actions, and told their stories by means of conventional gestures during the *scènes* and *pas d'action*. When Fokine developed his mimed dance and danced mime, the old dualism of dance and mime was largely eliminated, although twentieth-century choreographers still use the strictly academic technique as the firm basis of their design.

The best example of the older classical ballet is Petipa's *The Sleeping Beauty*. In the twentieth century such Ashton ballets as *Symphonic Variations* and *Monotones*, MacMillan's ballets with a theme, *Gloria* and *Requiem*, and Balanchine's many essays about music and, more importantly, his very clear interpretation of a myth, *Apollo*, are excellent examples of the style. *Apollo* was the first ballet to display a fresh way of looking at class-room technique for the communication of an ancient Greek legend. It taught many others how classical style could be adapted and developed. To create such a ballet, choreographers need to understand what type of character they are using and how the type of character will colour the dance movements.

Characters in classical ballet

When a choreographer creates a ballet based on ancient Greek or Roman myth and legend, or on medieval legends and the fairy tales derived from them, he can find inspiration for ways of acting out the story or theme by reading the works of authors such as Homer and Plato. These describe the appearance and behaviour of heroes, heroines, villains and other characters. They show what happens when an individual is confronted by fate. Such descriptions give a generalised picture of what such characters are and do. They behave much as do similar characters found in the epics of other nations. On the one side, they are all brave and honourable; if the epic has a happy ending they surmount every obstacle; if there is a tragic end, they succumb in an unequal fight. On the other side, the villains are truly evil and are equally well described.

The scholars of the Renaissance courts studied in depth the philosophy and dictates of classical authors and applied their knowledge to the education of courtiers, so that they would act and behave correctly in the new society. The most important field of study was that of courtly behaviour and manners so that the attention of everyone was focused round the king, prince or prelate. It was equally important to ensure that all would-be courtiers studied music, which in the fifteenth and sixteenth centuries included all the arts and muses. This required a knowledge of the theory of numbers and geometrical design, of singing and playing some musical instrument, of composing poems, of dancing, fencing and sword play, as well as of practising the fashionable sports and pastimes.

This study of the Muses in the widest sense was reflected in the work of such balletmasters as Beaujoyeulx, producer of the first *ballet de cour* and later by Beauchamps, dancing master to Louis XIV. The same types of generalised character continued and still appeared in Petipa's many ballets, Fokine's *Pavillon d'Armide*, Ashton's *Cinderella* and MacMillan's *Romeo and Juliet*. There are some glimpses of the same behaviour in MacMillan's *Mayerling*, although the manners and behaviour have deteriorated. The heroines of such ballets go hunting, practise archery, play lutes or mandolins, dance appropriate period dances and generally behave 'as to the manner born in aristocratic surroundings'. They arrive on stage in strict order of precedence, the noblest usually arriving last so that the lesser characters can look on in suitable admiration, whilst the servants (the *corps de ballet*) keep their distance. This acceptance of the usual forms of court etiquette was first developed in a particular social environment, and it is important to comply with it if a proper atmosphere is to be established for the action which is to take place.

Rules of behaviour

The need for classical dancers to study courtly behaviour is nowhere more important than in all *pas de deux*. The courtesies to be shown are seen at their best when Aurora dances with her Prince in the last act of *The Sleeping Beauty*. It is not merely the gracious bow they give each other before they begin, nor the even more gracious one when she submits to the prince, sinking to the ground with head bent low. She then places her hand in his and with his help gradually rises onto *pointe* until she poses triumphantly in *attitude*. The way he proffers his open hand before this difficult feat of balance draws attention to the vital part to be played by all heroes in classical ballet.

The *danseur* must complement and follow the lines drawn by the ballerina as she poses and dances. It is often the way he extends his hand to take hers and the way she responds that lead to the successful conclusion of a balance, lift or *pirouette*. It is not always understood that he does not only help her but has frequently to lead her into a movement. He can do this by guiding her with a strongly held forearm or firm hand clasp as she sustains a pose. He can steady her balance by holding his hands sufficiently close but not grasping her waist as she *pirouettes*, then grasp it firmly at the end of the turn, maybe to twist her into another pose. He must know how to lift or catch her in different ways from a static position or jump without any sign of strain. Nor must he step outside the dimension of the choreographic design both are making.

The ballerina has to behave as graciously and confidently as her partner. She must know how to give or take his hand and always to acknowledge his presence as an equal partner in the dance. Admittedly in many of Petipa's *pas de deux* he seems merely to be a porter. This is because Petipa was not interested in male dance and often left the *danseur* to arrange his own brief solo. But such a situation should not be allowed to occur because any casualness in the ballerina's behaviour destroys any attempt to convey style in the classical manner.

Among the best early examples of how hero and heroine should dance *pas de deux* are those in *Giselle* and *La Sylphide* where both have equal rights as dancers. A weak dancer playing Albrecht or James spoils the total effect. A more recent master of *pas de deux* is Ashton whose choreographic designs in ballets such as *Symphonic Variations*, *Cinderella*, *Scènes de Ballet* and *Ondine* reveal many different ways of displaying the spaciousness, dignity and grace of courtly behaviour. It is necessary to preserve this style and he does so despite the modernity of some of the movements.

Another important instance of courtly behaviour is when the hero has to lead the heroine into the dance. Is he merely to proffer his hand and lead her into a stately minuet? Is he to stand behind her, to take her right hand in his right and to lift it over her head while their clasped left hands stretch sideways before they move swiftly and diagonally into an allemande? Or is he to allow her to rest her left forearm on his right and to guide her round in an elegant mazurka — leading her, as it were, from the shoulder so that she always moves just in front of him? Such beautiful manners are quite unlike those of the ranch hands and their girls in De Mille's *Rodeo* or those in MacMillan's *Elite Syncopations*.

In addition to the courtesy the partners show to each other, there are also the courtesies that must be shown to the bystanders on stage during a *pas de deux* so that such reciprocation can help to focus the audience's attention on the context of the dance. The courtesies must also be exchanged between couples in a group dance. This is very important where there is a constant change of partners. There should be an acknowledgement on meeting and a 'thank you' on parting, no matter how brief.

The exchange of tiny glances that partners must practise in any *pas de deux* is artistically valuable and technically important. It helps them to find their centre of balance when working close together and also to counter-balance their weight when necessary. They must always be seen to have sufficient room in which to manoeuvre if they are to create a spaciousness for the most difficult changes in *épaulement* as pose follows pose. Room is obviously important when the ballerina is wearing a tutu, whose shape should not be distorted by a collision between the partners. It is equally important when she is wearing a soft tunic or one-piece tights and leotard. The lines made by the two dancers together must always have room to breathe and to be seen separately if the whole design is to flow. It is possibly the spaciousness of design that brings audiences again and again to Ashton's *Symphonic Variations* and *Monotones*, whose straighter and continuously moving lines require the dancers to draw them calmly and to fill the stage generously with movement. This could not be more different from the cruel flinging of Mary Vetsera's body by Rudolf in the *Mayerling pas de deux* with which MacMillan describes the Count's tragic mental state.

Technical characteristics

Classical dance in its purest form requires symmetry and balance. Each part of the body must be placed in a true relationship to the others and to the whole as the dance flows onwards. This requirement has its origins in Greek sculpture. Anyone seeing such works of sculpture for the first time cannot fail to note the harmonious line described through the perfectly proportioned bodies of the men and women portrayed. No matter from which angle they are viewed, these statues reveal that the head and limbs counter-balance each other round a central line running through the body so that each part is one with the whole picture. There is space, dimension and structure. All is open and alive for all to see.

If choreographers have had training in classical dance, they already have a large vocabulary of movement on which to call. Petipa divided movement into seven categories which other teachers have analysed further. If these definitions were put through a computer they would list five kinds of jumps, twenty-three *pas de bourrée*, seven *glissades* and so on. The technical structure of each step and pose is known and years of practice in hundreds of class-rooms have produced principles of calm and spacious movement. But technical descriptions only indicate the positions through which the feet and legs should move and at which moment they should co-ordinate with the arms as weight is transferred from one step and pose to the next. There are few, if any, suggestions of how individual movements can be linked together to achieve some expressive or rhythmic quality suitable to the style of dance required by the plot, theme and/or music. If choreographers wish to make their design more interesting they should attempt to give each step and pose some distinctive quality or unusual place in the design, which may or may not break the old conventions. As Fokine said: 'There can never be revolution in dance, only evolution, because the human body remains as it always has been, a living apparatus which can only move in certain well-defined ways.' Choreographers should remember that the descriptions in any dictionary of steps only indicate the beginning, passing through and end of a single item. There is no linkage, no indication of how to amalgamate one step with another and no indication of either rhythm or quality to make the movement come alive.

Giving quality to the movements

'Routine is the enemy of art' is the wisest remark for every artist to digest. Every choreographer should realise that the usual vocabulary of steps is only a beginning. The problem is how to link them so that they become like sentences in a play or poem. They must make physical, musical and, when necessary, dramatic sense. The sentences must have a rise and fall, an ability to flow onwards with pauses for breath, like full stops, or a moment's silence for the onlookers to assess what has just been stated and to understand its purpose and place in the design before the dance continues. These choreographic sentences, no matter how short or long, broad or narrow, high or low must make sense within the total pattern or movement traced on the stage. This pattern is made not only by the dancers' feet as they move over the surface but also by the dancers' bodies as they move through space. Their limbs, torsos and heads can make straight, angled or rounded lines, usually at one and the same time, according to the natural structure of the dancers' bones and how they are activated by the muscles. The choreographer must learn the natural functioning of the dancers' bodies in order to combine steps and poses in a way that gives quality to the whole.

If the dance design is to have physical, musical and, when necessary, dramatic sense, would-be choreographers should study how and why Petipa divided his steps into seven categories and then study some examples of how other choreographers have used his ideas.

The auxiliary or preparatory steps

Such steps as *glissades*, *chassés*, *pas de bourrée* and so on, form the links between the steps of elevation, *pirouettes* and poses. They are the verbs which should initiate the style of movement needed to sustain a ballet. For example: to move from one foot to two in any *glissade*, it can and should be when first studied a smooth gliding movement as it is when Albrecht gently draws Giselle to sit on the bench before telling her of his love. But it can also be very brisk and neat with a perfect close in 5th position as it is in many Bournonville ballets and Ashton's *Birthday Offering*. It can also be danced *sur les pointes* or become a spacious preparation into some *grand assemblé* or *saut de basque en tournant* as in many Petipa solos. If the *glissade* is too emphatic then the step of *grande élévation*, the highlight of a sentence, will lose its impact. Thus when using *glissades* the choreographer must decide whether they are to be darted and controlled by careful spacing to close in an elegant 5th position, or glided smoothly with a gentle rise and fall, or danced in such a way that they give impetus to propel the dancer upwards into the step of elevation.

The above remarks presuppose that the choreographer has carefully studied the various ways of using the feet. Do they merely glide on the surface as they do in *Les Patineurs*? Do they weigh heavily downwards as in MacMillan's *A Distant Drummer*, where the *pas marchés* become a military exercise of horrific quality?

It is when discussing the many ways in which *pas de bourrée* can be danced that the uses of the feet are widely exposed. Dancers easily understand how a series of swift *pas de bourrée courus* (i.e. running on the toes) as danced by the Queen of the Wilis in *Giselle*, differs from the same step performed *piqué* (i.e. each foot picked up sharply at each change of weight), as in many of Petipa's solos. But it is not always easy to decide which is the more appropriate, nor how the two ways mentioned can lead to other versions. For example, in her solo in Ashton's *Cinderella* the Winter Fairy moves across the stage in a series of *pas de bourrée en tournant à terre*, the feet weaving their in-and-out pattern as the arms flick to and fro sparkling with frost. In *Symphonic Variations*, the dancers perform *pas de bourrée piqués sur les pointes* very gently because they are marking the rhythmic beat as the soloist dances to the melodic phrase. This is an excellent example where both the overall and shorter phrase rhythms are explicitly brought to life by the dance design (see page 68).

One of the most beautiful uses of *pas de bourrée courus* is when Ashton places his *danseuse* in her partner's arms as she floats over the surface of the floor as if in a dream-like ecstasy. It is a movement he has used many times and which is perhaps seen at its best in the *pas de deux* to the *Meditation* from *Thaïs* created for Anthony Dowell and Antoinette Sibley; in *A Month in the Country* when Natalia dances with the Tutor to express her emotions; and in *Les Deux Pigeons* in the final *pas de deux*, when the Young Man has returned to The Girl and tenderly dances with her in his arms (see page 83).

It was this ability to display a ballerina's apparent weightlessness and sheer joy in dance that was so impressive when the Spirits of the Air danced in *Homage to the Queen*, Ashton's exquisite celebration of the 1952 Coronation which was danced by Margot Fonteyn and Michael Somes. Her feet scarcely touched the ground as she rose, descended, turned and floated to be held momentarily in some pose as a gesture of homage.

Steps of petite and grande élévation

It is not enough merely to consider how to perform the five jumps as a technical exercise. They must have quality given to them because their varying dimensions can add so much to the design. Certainly in the class-room those from two feet to two feet only go straight up and down in all *changements*, *soubresauts* and *entrechats* with both legs fully extended at the height of the jump. But such jumps can also travel some way forwards, backwards or sideways and can become sparklingly light when the knees are sharply bent upwards at the height of the jump. This is required of the Four Fairies, the Fairy Godmother and the Stars in Ashton's *Cinderella*. However if this way of jumping from two feet to two feet had not been combined with well picked-up *pas de bourrée piqués* and *relevés retirés* as well as extremely accurate, quick *ports de bras* with straighter and more angled than rounded arms, they would have seemed out of place.

When moving dancers from two feet to one in both open and closed *sissonnes*, the choreographer can make the movements dart over the floor as Aurora does in her final solo in *The Sleeping Beauty*. In *Les Patineurs* and *Les Rendezvous* Ashton makes his dancers travel upwards as well in an effort to show off their abilities to keep up with the music and beat each other to the exit.

Grands jetés en avant require a spring onwards from one foot to the other and can take on many forms. Are they to be sharply accented upwards with a hold on the downwards accent as they are in Ashton's version of the Act III *pas de quatre* in *Swan Lake*? Or are they to be softly stretched and so angled that they curve upwards and over before descending silently as in Fokine's *Les Sylphides*? These last *jetés* would be completely out of place in Lander's *Etudes* where a strong 'flick' outwards of the leading foot propels the dancer straight forwards through the air with little or no time to pause in *arabesque* on landing because the continuous repetition of this strong movement is intended to cover as much ground in as little time as possible. This gives an impression of speed which is so important in this interpretation of Czerny's finger exercises for the piano, and is quite alien to the soft rise and fall of the *Sylphides' jetés* danced to Chopin's romantic music in a woodland glade.

Grande and petite batterie

Petipa's suggestion that beats can add brilliance to the dance is nowhere better exemplified than in the *brisés volés* and *temps de poisson* of the Bluebird's solo in *The Sleeping Beauty* and other male solos from ballets by Bournonville. But it is not so easy to find good examples of his suggestion that *batterie* can lend wit except in the Blue Boy's *révoltades* in Ashton's *Les Patineurs*. But their witty performance depends on the soloist's own attitude to the fun. Is he really to appear as if tripping himself up and thus about to fall? Or is he to show how difficult he finds them? Ashton has also found a delicious use for the ordinary class-room *petits battements sur le cou de pied* when Cinderella parodies the Ugly Sisters' dancing lesson. There are many other instances of Ashton's witty beaten touches that may only become apparent after several viewings and are to be found in *Birthday Offering*, *Sylvia*, *La Fille Mal Gardée* and elsewhere.

Pirouettes

In the same way as steps of *batterie* and *grande élévation*, *pirouettes* are usually employed to add excitement. There are so many different ways of turning on one or two feet. Now that the teaching of *pirouettes* has become more scientific, dancers can attempt turning with the working leg held at many different angles, even changing the pose as they spin.

Since Legnani first danced the famous thirty-two *fouettés* in *Swan Lake*, it sometimes seems that choreographers lacking ideas for a spectacular finish to a solo, send the dancer spinning faster and faster round the stage, or set them centre stage and make them turn with increasingly difficult poses. In *Les Patineurs* they just spin happily in the snow.

The supporting leg can go on spinning on full *pointe* with that knee bent, as the working one is held in *arabesque* or *attitude* and finally sit on the floor. Whether the last two antics are viable depends entirely on the context. Such antics as performed by both girls and boys display how far technique has developed. Nevertheless they should have no place in pure classical ballets because they are largely acrobatic, and as such have a place only in certain modern works which discard the old conventions in order to display the athleticism and freedom of movement that today's choreographers use as part of their material.

Poses

As already stated, poses are the nouns in the dance phrases and act as statements (see page 67. It can be that magic moment in such dances as the Rose Adage in *The Sleeping Beauty* when Aurora triumphantly raises her hand from the Fourth Prince's grasp and holds the final *attitude* for several seconds revealing her complete command over the forces of gravity. There are hundreds of instances of this kind of pose created by many different choreographers. There is the moment in the Act II *pas de deux* of *Swan Lake* where Odette appears to fly away in an *arabesque* before Siegfried seizes her arms and draws her body close to his in an embrace. There are also the exciting poses that come at the end of some of Ashton's *pas de deux* as the two characters declare their love, for example, when Oberon cradles Titania in his arms at the end of *The Dream* and, even more excitingly, when Colas lifts Lise high on one arm at the end of their dance in Act II of *La Fille Mal Gardée* as if to crown her queen of the harvest.

In some modern classical ballets too little attention is paid to the momentary holding of a pose as the focus of a picture to sum up – as it were – what has gone before. Similarly, few choreographers make use of a sudden change of *épaulement* to make an emphatic statement. It is not easy to achieve this effect if they do not take into account the dimension and spacing of the steps as well as their particular quality, which must be in tune with the music if it is to make sense. A contradiction in style during this change of *épaulement* or alignment can distort the design. Nevertheless an unusual change of *épaulement* or alignment can add interest and draw attention to a dancer's statement. For example: the swift change from the *grand développé à la seconde* which Odile makes facing the audience and her sudden turn to *arabesque* when she looks straight into the kneeling Siegfried's eyes in the Act III *pas de deux* of *Swan Lake*; it is Odile's triumph for she knows she has won Siegfried's heart.

Even more exciting changes of *épaulement* can be found in Ashton's *Birthday Offering* where each soloist dances an old step at a new angle, without breaking the rules or older conventions of nineteenth-century ballet. He then gives an entirely new quality to the class-room exercise on which these *enchaînements* are based.

David Bintley, the Royal Ballet's new choreographer, also has a masterly touch when he creates exciting quick changes of *épaulement* in his 'classical' ballets. For example: in *Choros* he focuses attention on many ancient Greek dance rituals and accents the playful use of movement whilst at the same time showing that such warlike, athletic courtship and other activities are a wonderful game to be played by the performers. In *Consort Lessons* these quick changes of *épaulement* give much greater variety and dimension to the overall design particularly where the solo girl dances with four boys. More recently, in his *The Sons of Horus* he has found ways of incorporating the profiled attitudes and poses seen in ancient Egyptian designs with straight turned-in legs, elongated lines and angled arms, all in contrast to the turned-out legs and curving bodies of classical dance. As Ashton and MacMillan in many of their ballets, he has created a style appropriate to one particular ballet. Unless he chooses another ancient Egyptian theme he is unlikely to use the same style again.

Ports de bras

Petipa's remark that 'without *ports de bras* the dancer is dumb' is only one of the wise comments he made when working on his choreographic designs. Fokine echoed this remark when he said 'every step and pose is a gesture' (see page 58). De Valois summed up the ideas of these two great choreographers by saying: 'Only synchronisation of arms and legs will give symmetry to step and pose, strength to the jump, speed to the *pirouettes*, calm to the adage and spaciousness to the dance.'

To ensure that his audience would appreciate each sentence in his dance, Petipa usually repeated each at least twice and usually four times. But towards the end of the second or fourth repeat he made some small alteration in the *ports de bras* so that the dancer could move easily into the next sentence. He did this without ever losing sight of the contrasts he made between steps of each sequence because these were controlled by the particular rhythm, tempo and quality of the music. This is particularly noticeable in his variations for the Six Fairies in *The Sleeping Beauty*. Petipa clearly reflects in dance the gift that each Fairy brings to the Christening. The First Fairy is slow and gracious to denote Beauty; she encircles her face with her hand and displays the line of her arm (the traditional gesture for beauty). The Second Fairy brings Grace and dances slightly faster in such a way that she shows off the lines of her body as it faces forwards and then backwards (the traditional gesture). The Third Fairy dances slowly *sur les pointes* and uses conventional hand movements to show she brings the gift of Plenty, just as the godmother at a Russian christening scatters breadcrumbs over the cradle. The Fourth Fairy is a songbird bringing the gift of Language and flutters to and fro as she sings. The Fifth Fairy has fast stabbing movements of feet and arms to bring the gift of Energy. The Lilac Fairy is generously slow and controlled and taps her forehead because she is bringing the gift of Wisdom (the traditional gesture for wise). It is the gesture she uses later to make the Prince think what he must do to wake Aurora.

Similar contrasts in the qualities, musical tempi and phrasing within the classical style are found in Ashton's dances for the Four Seasons in *Cinderella*. Each step can be found in the classical vocabulary. Spring dances lightly and happily with fresh energy in the pale sunlight and soft breezes, with generous *ports de bras* to greet the dawn. Summer shows all the languor of a hot, breezeless day as the dancer lazily brushes her hand over her brow. Autumn is blown hither and thither by an ever-changing tempestuous wind. Winter sparkles in the frost (see page 79). The cold air is made even more apparent by the swift footwork when the entire cast jump lightly upwards away from the ground. Admittedly the décor and lighting help to create the illusion of changing seasons. But if Ashton had not made these very distinctive changes in his *ports de bras*, the seasonal differences would not have been so notable.

The above examples are only a few of those showing how conventional *ports de bras* can be changed. A study of Ashton's ways of using them, or of MacMillan's, reveal how unnecessary it is to keep passing the arms through 1st position. Nor is it necessary always to keep the arms rounded except in *arabesque*. Examples taken from both choreographers' works describe the particular feelings, moods and emotions of the characters their dancers are portraying. Arms flick to and fro as the Winter Fairy and the Stars of Ashton's *Cinderella* give the illusion of twinkling lights in the frosty air. The poignant shaking of the hands above upraised heads followed by the pressing downwards, outwards and then backwards of the arms make an overwhelming plea for pity in MacMillan's *Requiem*. The fact that the two leading English choreographers create so many unusual *ports de bras* as a means of expression is what has made so many Royal Ballet dancers so successful in ballets with a story. Coming from a country where the use of the appropriate word is more important than a gesture in daily life, both choreographers have resolved that words must be replaced by gestures within the choreographic design. Nowhere are they more telling than in Ashton's *Enigma Variations* where they explain the sympathy felt by Jaeger (the critic) for Elgar and his Wife or in *A Month in the Country* where Ashton communicates the growing feelings of love and frustration of the participants. Other profoundly moving gestures are to be found in MacMillan's *The Invitation* and particularly in his *Requiem* when he evokes a child's wonder of life in the solo, *Pie Jesu* (see page 136).

The pointes

The use of *pointes* as a delicate finishing touch is not always exploited by today's choreographers, who often use them to display their dancers' ability to 'get up and stay there' – come what may! The first 'stunt' of this kind in London occurred in a revue at the Hippodrome when the star dancer 'toe-tapped' up and down an escalator. In the next revue the star dancer 'charlestoned' on her *pointes*. Anyone using steel backs to their shoes can still do this. There is no light and shade and this way of using the *pointes* has nothing to do with giving a finishing touch to such dances as those for Petipa's Aurora and the Six Fairies in *The Sleeping Beauty* to make them seem lighter than air. Nor does it resemble the bravura footing of Kitri in the *Don Quixote pas de deux* or the passages in Ashton's *Ondine* where his ballerina appears to be floating through water. Nor can it be compared with the ballerina's dance in *Rhapsodie* where she wafts to and fro as if in a dream before breaking into her solo. The spacing of such steps on *pointe* is so minute and so fast that it is not possible to see the change of feet as one succeeds the other.

It is this same delicate use of *pointes* throughout Ashton's ballets which gives extra finesse to the *danseuses*' work. One of the most subtle finishing touches that *pointes* give is to Bottom in *The Dream* when he is transformed into an ass. Who but Ashton would have thought of giving this country yokel so delicate a movement? Yet how better to characterise his transformation into a 'dear little donkey trotting here and there' with dainty feet? (The words are from an old song.)

Pointes can and do have an enormous part to play in classical ballet because there are so many ways in which they can be used to give character and variety to a role. Some of them are to be found in *Checkmate* when the Red Pawns pick their way from square to square, whilst their Queen guides her King to his throne with tender steps.

Those movements are in direct contrast to the stronger, vicious and spacious *pointes* of the Black Queen and her Pawns. The *pointes* must not be thought of as a prop on which to balance the body, but as an extra dimension to make dramatic sense of a statement about the character on *pointes* and/or to relate in some way to the story or theme. Otherwise they are a mere technicality to be mastered with much patience and practice.

Following the rules of classical dance

As de Valois said in a lecture to teachers: 'It is better to have a rule to break than no rule at all if chaos is not to reign in the class-room or on the stage.'

A choreographer working in the classical style is wise to conform to the traditional principles and rules found valuable through years of experience. They are based on a refinement of the natural movements made by the bones and joints when activated by the muscles, tendons and ligaments found in any human body. The movements were and still are practised because they are designed to display the body as it moves to the best advantage from the audience's point of view. They were and still are designed to give that style of dance spaciousness, calm, balance and grace of form so that the lines drawn during the transition from one step and/or pose to another fills the available space in every dimension. In every *enchaînement* each step and/or pose must be given its appropriate value by way of beginning, climax and end so that its place is justified by its importance to the whole sentence. This does not mean that today's choreographers need follow the conventions laid down by the Renaissance scholars who were more interested in the physical ability and behaviour of courtiers. They were not creative artists but they were and still remain for the most part arbiters of technique and the niceties of perfect performance. The originality of so much of

Birthday Offering   Ashton's technical virtuosity (The Royal Ballet)

Ashton's and MacMillan's choreography for classical ballets lies in the way they follow the basic principles and rules in order to create an infinite variety of *enchaînements* from the traditional vocabulary of steps, and yet discard the conventions.

Choreographers who do not adhere strictly to the old conventions of court etiquette realise that their total design will flow more easily because their dancers' behaviour will appear more spontaneous and natural. For example: each soloist need not begin with a formal bow to a king or to the audience, nor end with another bow or considered pose; but such behaviour may be included if the choreographer wishes to locate dance in a particular century and probably a palace in which the story unfolds. Many new members of an audience have been known to object to the applause greeting the last bow. It breaks the continuity of the dance. Other practices that once held up the flow of the dance were the continual closing in 5th position before a new step and the continual moving of the arms through 1st position at every change of weight or during a *ports de bras*. This last convention is invaluable in early training because it helps to stabilise balance during the transfer from one foot to the other and is also valuable in such ballets as *Birthday Offering* as it echoes the period and style of Glazounov's music. But this would get very boring if used too often. Another old rule decreed that dancers never turned their backs on the audience, because all had to face the king, the centre of attention. The turn of a dancer's back can now become part of a beautiful line being made in a total picture. Today's dancers not only dance for an audience. They also dance for and with each other. And it is their response to each other's movements and their own enjoyment in dance that makes their behaviour appear natural and spontaneous even when they perform difficult technical feats.

It is perhaps not surprising that choreographers use the classical style for most abstract ballets. Even those basing their work on modern techniques seek to create a total picture with all the movements in harmony, as in ancient Greek sculptures. They must, therefore, ensure that the choreographic lines in their design flow through and round the centre of their dancers' bodies and that limbs and heads move in true co-ordination. They too wish to display their dancers' bodies at their fullest extension, therefore they must give them time, rhythm and space in which to move. Any untoward or awkward transition is immediately noticeable because it destroys the calm dignity that the human body needs if it is to be shown at its best. This does not mean that speed must be avoided, nor that the unexpected need offend the eye. A sudden change of *épaulement*, an unusual turn in-out of legs or arms, or quick jumps up and then down to the floor followed by a roll over or even a somersault can accentuate the particular place that unusual movement has in the whole design.

Swift changes in the dimensions covered in any linear design are nowhere more obvious than in Ashton's five abstract ballets and his example is now being followed by David Bintley in his *Choros* and *Consort Lessons*. In fact such unusual movements often arouse the audience to gentle laughter as swift changes add a touch of humour as two or more dancers compete to capture the attention of both the audience and their colleagues.

Classical dance patterns

In classical ballet the patterns and groupings delineated by the dancers' bodies are usually symmetrical and evenly balanced over the whole stage. This symmetry of design comes with the nature of this style of dance and its historical development. Technically each movement emanates from and is circled round a centre line of balance. Therefore in daily training it is customary for each exercise to be performed to the left and right, forwards and backwards. But even if a choreographer breaks such regularity when setting a classical ballet he usually balances the pattern made on the floor in one *enchaînement* by another moving in the opposite direction. This balancing of floor patterns is also matched by the rise and fall of the dancers' bodies, heads and arms. It is very noticeable in Petipa's ballets, particularly in all the *corps de ballet* work of *The Sleeping Beauty*. Ashton and MacMillan adopt the same practice in their ballets which can be called classical in the court meaning of the term and whenever the music used is composed according to the formulae for classical composition. They do this even though they may break the conventions from time to time. They do it because they know the audience is watching a constantly evolving picture which is being drawn on, over, across and above a flat stage in front of a background. They know they must fill the empty space with movement, whether there is scenery in the background or where the costumes are at their simplest and the background merely a hint of some venue as, for example, in *Symphonic Variations* or *Requiem*, or even just shafts of light as in *Monotones*.

It is useful for would-be choreographers to study the historical development of classical style so that they may stage a ballet in a traditional way when it has a story firmly linked to a particular time and place. When the members of the newly founded French academies laid down rules for all artists at the court of Louis XIV, they had to conform whether they were painters, sculptors or designers of scenery, props and tapestries. The rules stated that artistic works had to be inspired by the ancient Greek arts, be symmetrical, properly proportioned and balanced round a centre. These edicts were particularly important for all concerned in the opera-ballets in which the king himself frequently appeared at the climax of the action. To prove his importance and so that his entrance was emphasised all entered in order of precedence. He was thus the focus for all performers as well as spectators. His position is now occupied by the ballerina and her partner or a soloist. It should be noted that a similar order of precedence exists in Ashton's *Scènes de Ballet* as in Petipa's *The Sleeping Beauty* which was supposed to be an evocation of a court ballet at the time of Louis XIV.

However, when ballets were performed for the public, professional dancers took the place of courtiers and technical innovations had to be made. The dancers now appeared on a stage before a wide audience and the focus of their attention changed to the whole audience or to the most important performers. They had to adapt their movements to cover a larger space which was like a box with one side only being open to public gaze. They had to pay greater attention to the placing of each step and pose within the new framework. Much time was spent in the formulation of rules to lay down the alignments and *épaulements* which would best display each movement from the audience's point of view. These rules still hold good for choreographers who work in the classical medium and the wise ones never neglect them. If they do, their design loses the calm spaciousness which the style demands, no matter how fast or slow the dance. For example: by making his six dancers appear equally important in *Symphonic Variations* Ashton was the first to break away from the convention of making a ballerina the focus of attention. (He repeated this idea for the six dancers in *Monotones I and II*.)

Nevertheless his choreographic plan is so designed that each movement of every dancer, whether as an individual or part of the group, is co-ordinated with the others so that it fits correctly into the overall pattern and within the space allotted by stage,

Swan Lake   The classico-romantic
ballet of Ivanov and Petipa
Right: Odette's arabesque as Swan;
below: Odile's arabesque as
enchantress (Yvette Chauviré, Erik
Bruhn; Merle Park, Rudolf Nureyev)

wings and backcloth which – in *Symphonic Variations* – delicately echoes the curving lines of the dance.

The fact that dancers acquired more space within which to move also meant that all *terre à terre* steps could cover more ground. The floor patterns ceased to be confined to the curved, angled or straight lines decreed by the older rules which proposed that certain geometrical figures had great significance. They could only be understood by those educated as courtiers. For example: certain dances had to be composed with two sections only, such as the earliest minuets, which made the shape of a 'Z', i.e. a diagonally straight line with an acute angle at each end. Later minuets drew the shape of an 'S' as the footwork began to flow more easily.

The strictly geometrical pattern of dance is still very important if the musical score retains a traditional structure. Perhaps the best example for choreographers to study is Petipa's work for the *corps de ballet*, particularly in *La Bayadère* (Scene of the Shades). As the thirty-six girls enter one by one down the ramp at the back of the stage and move into six straight lines across the stage until it is completely filled, there is one continually progressing line of *arabesques* and *ports de bras*. This demonstrates what can be done with two simple movements to hold an audience's attention. Later the mass of dancers merely moves upstage *sur les pointes* to a pose and further *ports de bras*, then returns downstage to another slowly unfolding set of *ports de bras* and *arabesques*. It is when this mass of dancers divides and moves to the sides that the open space available for dancing is exposed for the first time. Before this the slow-moving dancers in their wide spreading tutus and veiled arms have hidden it from view. Its exposure prepares the audience for the brilliant solos to follow.

When Marie Camargo shortened her skirts and removed the heels from her shoes, jumps and *batterie* first entered the vocabulary. These lent brilliance to the footwork which became more intricate and thus more interesting. As music and musical instruments developed and became more flexible, so did the dance. Not only were dancing masters expected to follow their own rules of dance but they also had to conform to the rules of the Académie Royale de Musique. Later, the introduction of *pointes* and the 'ballerina' skirt led to the dominant role of the ballerina at the expense of the male dancer and this brought further changes in the patterns. Many more recent innovations in costume have led to today's all-over leotard and tights which has not only given dancers complete freedom of movement but has given choreographers freedom to design as they will without constricting rules and conventions. But such apparent freedom must be controlled if the dance is to remain wthin the limits of the true classical style.

Means of expression – conventional mime

An important step in the development of classical ballet for storytelling came with John Weaver's staging of *The Loves of Mars and Venus* (London 1717). He did away with actors and singers to tell the story as had happened hitherto. He insisted that his dancers told their own story by using the many conventional gestures familiar to theatregoers throughout Europe. He explained the gestures in the libretto he prepared for his audience. As a Greek and Latin scholar he had found them described in the works of ancient authors who wrote about the moods, emotions and actions of all the actors involved in their dramas. By 1717 these gestures were accepted practice by actors to reinforce the meaning of the words spoken and particularly by members

Scènes de Ballet   Ashton and the older classical style
The Ballerina is the focus of attention (Antoinette Sibley, Anthony Dowell and The Royal Ballet)

of the commedia dell'arte travelling troupes who produced mime plays. In these the expert gestures and extemporised playing of easily recognised characters in certain stock situations were understood by audiences everywhere no matter what the native language because the gestures were so explicit.

These gestures were first listed by monks in the tenth century. They described some four hundred used by monks and nuns of certain religious orders during the hours of silence. Some can be seen in religious paintings, particularly those of the Virgin Mary, the Saints and the Angels. Some actors today, notably Sir John Gielgud, use them when playing in classical drama and some eighty are still part of a dancer's means of telling a story in classical style. They have become part of the spacious *ports de bras* used during the dance.

They conform to the same technical rules as *ports de bras* and must appear to pass through the centre line of the arm from shoulder to finger-tips and move within the two circles drawn by the elbows and hands. Two of the best examples occur when the Lilac Fairy casts the spell that sends Aurora to sleep in *The Sleeping Beauty* ('Until a prince comes, sees her, falls in love and kisses her awake.') and when Siegfried swears to marry and save Odette after she has told him how the wicked Von Rothbart turned her into a Swan (*Swan Lake*, Act II).

Fokine broke down the artificial practice created by earlier choreographers and his dancers acted as they danced. He felt that to stop the dance and make gestures, no matter how elegantly, destroyed the flow and the ability of the dancers to communicate expressively the meaning of their movements. He began by including some conventional gestures within the *ports de bras* of *Les Sylphides* and *Le Carnaval*. He further developed what he called his danced mime or mimed dance in *The Firebird* and above all in *Petrushka*. It is in this field that Ashton and MacMillan have made many innovations in those of their ballets that describe very subtle relationships, feelings and emotions such as *A Month in the Country* and *Enigma Variations*, *The Invitation* and *Mayerling*. In the last, MacMillan's choreography makes Bratfisch, the prince's coachman, appear as the only sympathetic yet helpless onlooker at the sordid proceedings. Bratfisch attempts to entertain the doomed couple at the last meeting before their death and his sorrow as he comes to the graveside of the murdered heroine are an object lesson in understatement. So explicit are the tiny gestures and the perfect timing of exits and entrances that the audience is forced to recognise the personal tragedy of a love that spoke no words.

Although MacMillan's choreography for both the above ballets is based on classical technique, it in no way conforms to the old school of dance or conventional mime. To portray specific characters, whether imagined or real (some were known to members of the audience at the first performance of *Enigma Variations* and *Isadora*), the would-be choreographer can use classical dance as a firm base but must pay more attention to his characters as particular individuals. They live and work in a more varied, often plebeian, environment than that of courtiers in the palace of a prince. The latter, after all, was the stereotype setting for all classical ballet until 1789, the year of the French Revolution. *La Fille Mal Gardée* of 1789 was the first ballet to display the lives and loves of peasants and farmers. Even the popularity of these lesser mortals could not drive aristocrats completely from the stage, particularly in those countries where major theatres continued to be subsidised by Royal Treasuries who largely dictated what choreographers could produce.

The style of *demi-caractère* ballet

The *demi-caractère* style has its roots in classical technique, but must be coloured by more clearly defined and individual movements which allow the dancers to show they are playing the part of some character who has some claim to live in the real world and therefore can be recognised as such. In other words they usually, 'dance classically from their feet to the waist and above that are free to express themselves as people of more definite behaviour, work, play and age' (de Valois in a lecture to teachers, 1947).

The head, body and arms of the characters portrayed should show the status they have in the society to which they belong whether it is rural, urban or fantastic, as well as their behaviour, customs, work or play. Dauberval's *La Fille Mal Gardé* (1789) was the first ballet in this style. Dauberval's exclusion from the Acadmie Royale (later the Paris Opera) was justified by those in charge because they felt his idea of making farmers, peasants and the like the heroes and heroines of his ballets was beneath the dignity of an opera house whose stage had hitherto been occupied with the deeds of noble heroes, heroines and courts. Bournonville coloured his ballets with movements characteristic of many different personalities and nationalities. In his particular style of *demi-caractère* dance he used classical footwork for most of the time but, from the waist upwards through the body, arms and head, he tried to convey how his performers worked and played in the environment to which they belonged. For example: in *Napoli* they were Italian, in *Far from Denmark* they were Danes influenced by the dance of South America.

This way of creating more plebeian characters is fully demonstrated in Ashton's comic masterpiece *La Fille Mal Gardée*, where this style of dance is shown in two different aspects, the light-hearted yet technically highly expert dancing of Lise and Colas and the comically eccentric work of Alain and the Cock and Hens. Their dance is very different from the work of Petipa, whose suggestion of *demi-caractère* is seen when the Songbird and Bluebird dance in *The Sleeping Beauty*, where the fluttering of the hands is meant to indicate that birds fly and sing. Ashton's Cock and Hens come straight from the farmyard and not the Imperial Ballet. They squawk and scratch with unturned-out feet in *temps levés* and *batterie*, elbows flapping and heads pecking and poking. Petipa's ideas about birds were followed by Ivanov's Odette in *Swan Lake* and later in Fokine's unforgettable *The Dying Swan* for Anna Pavlova. But by the time Fokine produced *The Firebird* he had developed his mimed dance much further. It had become the most important part of his choreography. His Firebird flew and still flies in all her glory before being trapped pitifully in the arms of the Tsarevich. Her release sends her soaring in *grands jetés en avant* through the magic garden. This flight of the magic bird held and still holds audiences spellbound.

Ashton's version of *La Fille Mal Gardée* is a perfect twentieth-century example of *demi-caractère* ballet. So are de Valois' *The Rake's Progress*, Cranko's *Pineapple Poll* and Robbins' *The Concert*.

However despite the great variety of *demi-caractère* ballets staged since 1789 there appear to be only three main sources of gesture which contribute to a particular style for a particular ballet. These have led to the same stereotyping of characters as happens in classical ballet. The three sources are:

Firstly the secular, moral and emotional behaviour of characters found in rural or urban communities;

Secondly the traditional dances and customs of a particular country that can give local colour and atmosphere to a plot or theme;

Thirdly gestures and behaviour from work activities in rural areas (landowners, farmers and peasants) or in urban areas (merchants, innkeepers and so on) or from the professions (army, navy, medicine, law).

Characters in *demi-caractère* ballets

Literally translated *demi-caractère* means 'half character', but that gives little understanding of its implications in ballet. It should describe how the characters, usually non-aristocratic or less educated, express moods, emotions and actions as they would in real life. The types of character and the plots in which they play have existed since the Dorian mimes first began to lay the foundations of the theatre. The art of mime was developed by the commedia dell'arte and is still being developed by such artists as Marcel Marceau and the mime theatres of Poland and Czechoslovakia.

Actors in travelling companies used to set up their stage in a town or village, mix among the inhabitants, watching and listening to the local news, gossip and scandal.

They became adept at portraying well-known types such as the domineering wife, her hen-pecked husband, the poor widow anxious to get a son or daughter wed, the miser, the guardian or the severe nurse and at spotting any odd person or antics. They were also fond of aping the grand manners of servants to aristocratic households and rich farmers. Each player in these groups was engaged for his or her ability to perform one type of role, therefore the playing was predictable because there was a particular way of acting out the various situations. These often required jokes, tricks and special ploys, all of which were performed in dumb show, something at which the great mimes Grock and Charlie Chaplin were expert.

Foremost amongst the travelling players were the Serious Lovers who were to become the *danseurs nobles* and ballerinas of classical ballet, because they were always noble heroes and heroines. Their two servants, known as the Comic Lovers or, later, Harlequin and Columbine, were to become the *danseurs classiques* or *demi-caractère* dancers.

In ancient Greek myth Harlequin made his first appearance as Hermes (or Mercury), the messenger of the gods and himself the god of all animals and travellers. This heritage gave and still attributes to him the ability to move fast, avoiding all obstacles, to do his master's bidding. When in trouble he could, like a god, make himself invisible or turn himself into an animal.

Shakespeare's Puck, as envisaged by Ashton in *The Dream*, is a wonderful example of Harlequin's role. It was the aspect of Harlequin as servant that intrigued Massine, who employed it in his own portrayal of the factotums, bar-tenders and servants in several works. Ashton demonstrated Harlequin's technical expertise when he was transformed into Colas, a farmer, dancing with his shepherd's crook. Ashton did the same when Daphnis competed for Chloë's attention in his interpretation of Ravel's *Daphnis and Chloë*. When the character of Harlequin, the Comic Lover, had become familiar in England he was quickly promoted to lead the pantomimes; nowhere in ballet does he rise to more commanding heights than as Captain Belaye in Cranko's *Pineapple Poll*, where he takes on the superior airs and manners of the British Navy and becomes the apple of every girl's eye.

Columbine too started life as a servant of the gods and gradually rose in rank from waiting on the aristocracy to conspiring with Harlequin in such ballets as *The Good-Humoured Ladies*, where the two of them appear as serving maid and waiter. Columbine became Mother Simone's daughter, Lise, in *La Fille Mal Gardée* where she makes butter, churns and helps to spin. She is also there as the inquisitive fun-loving Swanhilda in *Coppélia* and displays a humble origin in Cranko's *Pineapple Poll*.

She is not, however, always the fun-loving Columbine of Fokine's *Carnaval*. In de Valois' *The Rake's Progress* she confirms her eighteenth-century origin as an innocent serving wench whom the Rake has dallied with and then discarded. Columbine is rarely seen in so tragic a role. That is why she elicits so much sympathy. She is the only decent character among the money-grabbers and hangers-on surrounding the Rake. Her role has the same sobering effect on the atmosphere of the ballet as that of Bratfisch, the Count's valet, in *Mayerling*.

Harlequin, in his earlier embodiment as Hermes, was the god of animals and this idea has been another valuable source of choreographic material. Ashton's design for Pepe, the dog, in *The Wedding Bouquet* was bettered when he created the Town and Bad Mice, Pigling Bland and the other animals in the film *The Tales of Beatrix Potter*. He used all the steps in the classical vocabulary named after Harlequin's early ability as dancer-acrobat to change himself into an animal. Amongst the steps are *sauts de carpe*, *temps de poisson*, *pas de cheval* and so on. From the same source come such diverse creatures as Massine's poodles in *La Boutique Fantasque*, a delicious pair of goats in Ashton's *Sylvia* and of course the squawking Cock and Hens in *La Fille Mal Gardée*.

It was an easy step for Ashton to respond to the sadness attending the closure of the Covent Garden Market in central London. His delicious *Pas des Légumes* performed at a special performance to mark the market's passing brought to mind the long history not only of the 'fruit and veg', but also of Harlequin, Columbine and their colleagues of the commedia dell'arte, inhabitants for many years of the Theatre Royal, Drury Lane, and the King's Theatre, Drury Lane, where the first *ballets d'action* were staged.

Giving quality to the dance through music, patterns and traditions

One of the most successful ways of giving a different quality to the steps and poses of classical dance and of transforming them into *demi-caractère* style is to relate them intimately to appropriate music. Every country has its own way of performing the traditional dances which go hand in hand with certain musical characteristics. Choreographers should note the particular relationships between steps and notes, *enchaînements* and phrases and how strong or weak beats affect the rhythm. They cannot be too strict about this relationship, for the score, whether commissioned or arranged, will only give some flavour of the traditional ways of singing and dancing. This can be easily recognised if Bizet's music for *Carmen* is compared with De Falla's for *The Three-Cornered Hat*. Yet the former has sufficient Spanish flavour, as does the Minkus score for *Don Quixote*, for audiences to believe that characters really would perform in the way they do to the kind of music provided.

When Dauberval removed to Bordeaux, the audience, like those elsewhere in France, was largely unaware of the grandeur of aristocratic entertainment. It welcomed the new ideas in *La Fille Mal Gardée* because the characters portrayed were familiar and were living in the farms and vineyards. Dauberval is said to have borrowed steps and gestures from such people to give his ballet greater reality. By so doing he originated a style of dance which owed its liveliness to the way such people behaved and danced in real life. Even so, he did not fully dispense with the technique of the classical school. He realised, as did later choreographers, that the steps and patterns of such material had to be properly displayed to the audience, not just danced for themselves. In other words he opened up the circles, squares and longways sets to show what gave rhythm and life to the movements.

It is this opening up and exposure of traditional dance that is so important when choreographers attempt to give a realistic atmosphere to the style and expression of their work. They should remember that they are suggesting and not giving the actual location. In real life the onlookers are part of the activity and usually join in. In ballets such as *Petrushka* and *Rodeo* they are wandering around, watching and occasionally responding to the dancers' efforts. But audiences sitting and watching can only join in the fun in their imagination and if the dancers are sufficiently out-going.

Choreographers like Bournonville often borrowed from regional dancing, which he eagerly studied wherever he travelled. It is useful for would-be choreographers to examine his ballets and discover that he mostly set them in countries possessing easily recognised characteristics. If his dances are compared with those derived from similar sources by later choreographers, Bournonville's generalisations of style become evident. The most outstanding are Scottish, Italian and Spanish.

Scottish style

The Royal Danish Ballet's production of *La Sylphide* is evidence of Bournonville's imaginative use of the Scot's quick light footwork and 'capers' as well as the very distinctive Highland *ports de bras*, which help the dancer to sustain balance. To these features he added purely classical *batterie, grands jetés en avant* and *en attitude, cabrioles* and quick *glissades* into *échappés à la seconde* and swift changes of *épaulement*. He also took care to make the patterns of his dances as interesting as in Scottish country dance. Another example of this stereotyped Scottish style is danced by Swanhilda in *Coppélia*. Much later, Ashton made a delightful caricature of it in his 'Scottish Rhapsody' in *Façade*. Yet oddly enough when Massine staged his *Donald of the Burthens* with the help of a Scottish expert to guide him through the traditional steps and figures it was not a success, possibly because too much reliance was placed on authenticity and not enough on the sheer fantasy of the story.

In his Scottish dances Bournonville highlighted the Highland characteristic of an upwards lift from the floor on the first beat of a bar whereas in English and French dance the movement is downwards. This makes the Scottish footwork look very light and easy particularly as it is allied to the steps of *petit* and *grand allegro* he also used. Another important feature is the absolute co-ordination of the arms as they change in the *ports de bras*, often moving through the 1st position. The change usually occurs on the first beat of a bar or phrase, which eliminates any fussiness when the footwork is intricate. Ashton maintained these formal changes in his frivolous 'Scottish Rhapsody'.

Italian style

Bournonville's *Napoli* is an absolute feast of Italian styled *demi-caractère* dance which comes to a superb conclusion during the wedding celebration of the hero and heroine. The whole cast muster in the market place before breaking into extravagant variations of the tarantella. Legs fly over tambourines held steady by one or the other partner. Round they spin, arms clasping each other's waists. Boy chases girl and catches her in a fond embrace without pausing as they cover the stage with footwork of a speed rarely seen elsewhere. Bournonville's *Flower Festival* is a slower, slightly more classical variation, as was Petipa's Neapolitan Dance in *Swan Lake*. Massine's quicker more set version of the tarantella in *La Boutique Fantasque* shows exactly the same features as those listed above.

Most traditional Italian dances are performed to a 3/4 or 6/8 time signature, the tarantella or salterello being recognised everywhere as being the most typical of the country as a whole. These both include many steps with the so-called 'dotted' rhythm i.e. in 3/4 the dancer steps on the first beat, holds on the second and briefly takes weight on the other foot on the third before stepping onwards. If this is danced to 6/8 it leads to the very swift footwork needed for Massine's tarantella and Ashton's version of the Italian *pas de deux* in *Swan Lake*, a miracle of timing and quick changes of *épaulement*. This type of dancing to a 'dotted rhythm' also leads to many steps where the dancers hop continuously on one leg holding the other firmly in *attitude devant, retirée*, or stretched backwards. Like Scottish *ports de bras*, those of Italy are very simple, the arms changing places after each sequence of dotted steps or hops. As traditional Italian dances are often sung, the performers pose solemnly for a second or two at the end of each phrase. This was a feature widely used by nineteenth-century Italian balletmasters and by Bournonville. But the latter's pause was often to hold the dancers in perfect 5th positions of both arms and feet.

Spanish style

The stereotyped Spanish style is possibly seen at its best in Petipa's *Don Quixote*, most particularly in the famous *pas de deux* for the ballerina and her partner. The tone is set by the continual use of the pose with head held high, back slightly arched, arms in closed 4th or a stretch fully upwards in 5th *sur les pointes* for Kitri or on *demi-pointes* for Basil. The brilliant bravura variation when Kitri springs lightly forwards *sur les pointes* whilst fanning herself and Basil attempts to make his zapateado (heel-tapping) appear authentic by the slightly crouching pose of his body, add even greater panache to their efforts. Swanhilda strikes similar poses with her mantilla and fan in *Coppélia* and so do the Spanish dancers in *Swan Lake*. However Massine in *The Three-Cornered Hat* took an entirely different view. His ballet is not *demi-caractère*. His choreography is firmly based on the authentic folk and flamenco dances he studied in Spain. His work must, therefore, be considered as one of the very few character/national ballets of its time, like the Russian ballets of Fokine.

Elsewhere reference has been made to the difference between Spanish style and flamenco style (see page 59) which belongs to the Spanish gipsies from whom has also developed what is known as gipsy character dance. There is however a third style of Spanish dance known as Spanish Court dance. This developed after the French Revolution of 1789 when many French dancing masters fled to Spain to become dancing masters to the aristocratic families. This led to a courtly style of social dance which Petipa studied and taught for some six years in Madrid before returning to St. Petersburg as balletmaster. His Spanish dance has therefore many authentic features seen through the eyes of a master classical teacher. Amongst the most notable are the poses finishing each musical phrase and the careful relation of the well-marked beats on heels to the beats of the music. The poses come as pauses at the end of each sequence, the dancer then changing position before beginning a new phrase, as if the guitarist were resting his fingers for a moment. The steps also diminish or broaden as the tunes grow softer or louder. But Petipa kept to well-defined limits of courtly behaviour and never fell into an extravagant style, even in the market place scene of *Don Quixote*.

Hungarian style

Towards the end of his life Petipa made much more use of *demi-caractère* elements in his work and strengthened the characteristics of the steps he used. He incorporated many Hungarian features in his production of *Raymonda* (last Act). He showed how intimately the traditional could influence the dances for his *corps de ballet*. Couples enter high-booted in an elaborate but genuinely traditional promenade. The working leg is thrust outwards on the first beat of a bar, heels click and stamp to accent the appropriate beats. Although the solo *danseuses* perform *sur les pointes*, they still mark the appropriate beats by stabbing their toes into the floor, i.e. they dance a series of *retirés passés* forwards or backwards without descending and use typical Hungarian *ports de bras*. These are also strongly accented as the arms straighten into 2nd position before being bent, with hands sometimes clasped behind the head, sometimes placed akimbo on the waist or sometimes with one on the waist and the other behind the large bow at the back of the head-dress. The *danseuses* perform some of the traditional steps such as the sideways moving *pas de bourrée* danced *sur les pointes* and the sideways *cabriole* rarely used in classical ballet.

The unusual feature of traditional Hungarian style is the strong distinction made between the two parts of most folk dances. They usually start with a promenade kept to a strictly slow tempo (the lassu) and then break into an extremely fast movement of turns, *pas de bourrée* and very controlled hops (the friss). It is this strong contrast between the two parts which is so important to maintain whether the dances are in *demi-caractère* or character (authentic) style. This contrast was used by Petipa to great advantage and demands a very musical dancer to display his brilliant choreography in *Raymonda*.

Oriental styles

Some of the most fascinating *demi-caractère* ballets are those where the choreographer has sought inspiration from oriental dance. This can be fairly easy to achieve because a brief study of ancient Egyptian friezes shows exactly how to adapt the movements depicted to the turned-out legs of classical dance. Petipa attempted this in *The Daughter of Pharaoh*. This type of choreography was taken up by later music-hall acts whose very eccentric soft shoe, sand dances before a background of pyramids and palm trees aroused much laughter. However when Fokine staged *A Night of Egypt* (later *Cleopatra*) he went a great deal further and developed a more particular Eastern style inspired by the performance of some Siamese dancers. He started by sketching numerous frescoes and statuettes he found in the Hermitage Museum, Leningrad. From such ideas he formed dances which did away with *pointes* but retained much of the classical footwork which he co-ordinated with the less familiar action of the arms and hands. Thus the angular and straight lines drawn by the legs were also drawn simultaneously by the arms and hands, which were allowed to cross the centre line of the body, very often with a twist sideways at the waist. This made the dancers appear as if they were a moving frieze. Something that David Bintley was also to achieve later in his *Sons of Horus* (1985).

Ashton too has created two oriental styled ballets in which the delicacy of the hands and arms drew attention to the way such subtle movements can take the place of words. His interest in *ports de bras* nearly always produces something new to say, whether it is to tell a story, describe the characters and/or create a style exclusive to one work.

Japanese The first of Ashton's ballets in oriental style was *Madame Chrysanthème*, in which he utilised many traditional Japanese gestures made more fascinating by emphasis of his dainty ballerina's footwork. Elaine Fifield did not always keep her feet fully pointed nor knees stretched, even when on *pointe*. At times the supporting leg would bend when on balance, whilst the working one was also bent with the foot turned up at the ankle during certain poses, or when performing a *rond de jambe en dehors* or *en dedans* during the *pas de deux*.

MacMillan created a very strong style of Japanese *demi-caractère* dance in *Rituals*. In the first scene he showed how men and boys prepared for combat and self-defence. This was followed by a wedding staged as if the Bride and Groom were being manipulated as puppets by a group of servants, a particular Japanese theatrical tradition. The final scene was a formal celebration and prayer for a wife giving birth. The movements were strongly influenced by the stylised Bugako players and were appropriate to each scene, but oddly enough the whole appeared too static, as if a series of Japanese prints was being paraded before the audience. At this time a MacMillan ballet was expected to be, above all, about dancing. The apparent ritualistic posing, although strongly performed and easy to understand, did not appeal in the same way as his *Song of the Earth*. Nevertheless the extraordinary use MacMillan made of the traditions of the Japanese theatre with its warlike ritual drills for self-defence showed how much more masculine his choreographic design was then becoming. This was no better reflected than in his creation of *A Distant Drummer* with its horrific theme of man's inhumanity to man, where ritual warlike movements were applied to the jack-booted soldiers of Nazi Germany.

Persian The second of Ashton's oriental ballets was *La Péri* (music by Dukas) for Margot Fonteyn and Michael Somes. Here La Péri's *ports de bras* were flowing and sensual yet almost innocent in order to express the magical vision Askender, the poet, was seeing in his dream. These gestures can be seen in many Persian miniatures, some of them at the British Museum. They are also part of certain styles of Indian dance where gestures are explicit in conveying the beauty of the world, of women and of love. In such dances physical contact between lovers rarely if ever takes place. Ashton broke this all-but-written law and communicated the exotic atmosphere of the dream but there was little to express the passion of love, which he would later convey in such works as *A Month in the Country*.

Chinese The most interesting of present-day ballets inspired by oriental sources is MacMillan's *Song of the Earth* (music by Mahler). It is an interpretation of and a parallel to the singing of seven Chinese poems about the ever transient phases in the life of Man. MacMillan has chosen to incorporate the delicate sometimes intricate turnings of the arms and hands used by the actor-dancers in the traditional Chinese theatre. But his choreography is no longer like that of earlier *demi-caractère* styles such as that of the Chinese dance in *The Nutcracker*. Together with the intricate and expressive *ports de bras* he allows his dancers' feet, legs and body to take on different shapes and lines as the design unfolds to interpret the words. The poems speak of Youth, of Beauty, of Love, of Parting and of Death, the last of which is not tragic but full of promise that life will be reborn. The solo man and woman are always accompanied by a masked figure known in China as 'the Eternal One' and in England as 'the Messenger of Death'. The words also speak of the joy and fun of friendship, of looking into a pool of knowledge, of drinking and lastly of a tender farewell. MacMillan has made this last song a welcome to the future as the three protagonists quietly and slowly come forwards, their hands linked, gradually raising their heads as if greeting a new day. Few ballets have so fully interpreted the deepest thoughts of a poet. The words speak a philosophy known and believed in China for many centuries.

Nautical styles

Although few characters from the professions appear to influence *demi-caractère* dance (their activities are usually confined to character works), the Navy and Army have regularly inspired choreographers. First comes the Navy. Versions of the traditional hornpipe danced by sailors of many nationalities are featured in many ballets because it is so descriptive of the very particular way in which seamen walk and do the many different jobs that have to be done on any kind of boat. The hornpipe is not exclusive to England, which many seem to think, even though Petipa in his ballet *The Daughter of Pharaoh* included a hornpipe to represent the Thames in a spectacular scene where the four greatest rivers of the world met 'under the sea'. Each country with a sailing history has its own version which differs only slightly from that

Song of the Earth   MacMillan's view of modern dance and interpretation of words
Left above: the boys' dance; left below: 'of Love'; above: 'The eternal round of man's love, life and death'
(Natalia Makarova, David Wall, Anthony Dowell and The Royal Ballet)

of others. The difference lies in the rhythm of the pipe tune to which it is danced. But much more can be made out of its well-recognised movements. A particularly fine example is that designed by de Valois for the Sailor in *The Rake's Progress*. It is easy to understand why he is in the madhouse. He is unsteady through drink and blind in one eye.

A brilliant example of variations on a hornpipe theme is to be found in Cranko's *Pineapple Poll*, which has very strong, even coarse elements when danced by the sailors before it is slightly refined by the gallant Captain Belaye. But when Poll, dressed in her sailor's uniform, proceeds to dance 'ship-shape' *sur les pointes*, with the Wives similarly equipped, it is easy to recognise the feminine touch that classical technique can give to their attempts at boat drill. Among the steps they perform are the traditional 'hauling up the anchor, paying out the rope, hoisting the flag, going on look-out after climbing the rigging' and, of course, 'taking the salute' – a little haphazardly.

Military style

Today very little military *demi-caractère* style exists in Western ballet except in such American works as Balanchine's *Stars and Stripes*, but it played a large part during the nineteenth century. It was then taken over by such excellent troupes as the Tiller and Jackson Girls who toured widely over Europe and America and later by the Drum Majorettes, who have also appeared in Balanchine's works. One glimpse of this well-disciplined style can be seen in Lichine's *Graduation Ball*, where both boys and girls march in formation and make other military manoeuvres. It is this aspect of military style that is well worth studying for the precision with which a battalion of soldiers makes patterns such as can be seen at the British ceremony of 'Trooping the Colour'. Something like this event was once staged at the Alhambra in the famous ballet *Soldiers of the Queen* at the height of the Boer War (1900). The scene represented an inspection and Grand March on the Queen's Parade, Aldershot. It was performed by the combined bands, drums and fifes, and some two hundred and fifty soldiers from thirty infantry regiments as well as a *corps de ballet* whose dances were arranged by Lucia Cormani. History does not relate what steps she used.

Balanchine employed every variety of *pas marchés* at every possible speed in *Stars and Stripes*. Every part of the foot was placed first on the flat and then up on *pointes*, and the working leg was raised to every possible height and angle. It was certainly a spectacular display of what dancers could do with their legs whilst merely marching, but the *ports de bras* were very limited and merely swung at the sides or sprang to attention.

Means of expression – occupational gesture

An English style of *demi-caractère* dance is not always very obvious except in the hornpipe and in Ashton's Harvest, Maypole and Morris Stick Dance in *La Fille Mal Gardée*, where the last two vary very little from the traditional versions. He rearranged the Stick Dance because of its vital link in the story. Fellow peasants carry Colas into Mother Simone's kitchen hidden in sheaves of corn so that he can meet Lise. They intend to carry out Lise and Colas by the same means. The trick does not work, but at least it leads to the hiding of Colas in Lise's bedroom and the awful discovery of the two of them together just as Alain has received the key and goes to claim his bride.

Many English stick dances, like those elsewhere, are believed to be ancient rituals in which the performers are enacting some job necessary for the well-being of the

The Rake's Progress   English National
Ballet and de Valois' interpretation of
Hogarth's evils of the day
Right: the Betrayed Girl; below: the last
meeting in Bedlam (Margaret Barbieri;
Margaret Barbieri, Desmond Kelly)

community. Such dances are the source of 'occupational gesture' (mime) and use movements which describe a certain work process. It is probably not realised how English this type of gesture has become and can be seen in many English ballets. It is not formally structured as it is in the ballets of other countries where choreographers are more likely to present the traditional dance itself, slightly adapted for the stage with the footwork more complicated. That is if they are creating a *demi-caractère* and not a national ballet (see page 120).

A wonderful example of an English *demi-caractère* dance is that of de Valois for the Betrayed Girl in *The Rake's Progress*. Here in the front cloth she is seen at her embroidery, sadly waiting and earning her living to pay off the Rake's debts. In and out goes the needle, the body, head and foot follow the direction of the hand as it pulls the thread through the canvas. She sighs, pauses, then in and out goes the needle again and again. The whole dance is controlled in rhythm, gesture and pattern as in all English folk dance. It also conveys the mood and emotions of the Girl, a very rare happening in true folk dance. The participants in folk dance can and certainly do show elation. In *La Fille Mal Gardée* Mother Simone does this when she triumphantly finishes her Clog Dance on the arms of her more graceful neighbours, just as all the guests but Alain do after the Betrothal and they all dance out, arms linked to celebrate.

The gestures of such pastoral characters as Lise and Colas in *La Fille Mal Gardée* have already been noted (see page 100) as well as that of Lise churning and helping her Mother to spin. But the conventional gesture 'to spin' has often been used in ballet. In *The Sleeping Beauty* Carabosse shows Aurora what a spindle is for and Aurora later shows how she can use it before she pricks her finger. In *Giselle*, Giselle shows Bathilde how she works. There are many instances of this use of the single gesture for spinning or threading a needle and making a stitch or two which are easily understood and recognised by an audience. A careful study of the gestures of the characters in *The Rake's Progress* reveal the trades of the tailor, jockey, dancing-master, gambler and others.

There are many kinds of occupation from which choreographers can and do borrow. These can roughly be classified as coming from work, hobbies and pastimes. The activity involved may be heavy or light or something with a specialised technique. For example, there is a very great deal of difference between sawing a large log by hand and stitching, or between playing a game of tennis and a game of cards. Embroidery requires a specialised technique, so does ice skating. In deciding to use a particular occupational process in his design a choreographer has four considerations:

1 He must decide the general outline of the process as he sees it in terms of movement. Traditionally every hornpipe begins as the sailors come on deck and dance figures-of-eight round the bollards before setting to work. Every harvest dance begins with the workers circling the field before moving into a straight line and beginning to reap.

2 He must select and contrast the strong and weak or tensed and relaxed movements in order to give them tempo, rhythm and expressive quality. The second step of every hornpipe is 'hauling up the anchor': the sailors stand one behind the other in line, bend down, grasp the rope with both hands, haul it backwards and then relax a moment before repeating the grasp and haul. To sweep a floor the broom must be firmly but lightly used to push the dust forwards, then carefully brought backwards just off the floor before repeating the push. This is what Lise does in Mother Simone's kitchen in *La Fille Mal Gardée* and Cinderella in her kitchen before she dances with the broom.

3 He must balance the movements one against the other to give proportion and emphasis as well as dimension. Each gesture in a sequence must be carefully timed so that it is of proper value to the whole. Once the sailor has 'climbed the rigging', which is usually an energetic process, he 'looks out', remaining stationary except for a slight sway as the boat sails out of harbour. Lise's dance when she sweeps the floor before helping Mother Simone to spin is an excellent example of how the subtle timing of gesture can be and is helped by the appropriate choice of music.

4 He must include all the necessary details which will suggest the purpose of the gestures. There can be few better examples of how to include all the necessary details than in de Valois' dance for the Betrayed Girl in *The Rake's Progress*. Not only does it demonstrate the work process but also the mood and emotion of the dancer. This is also true of occupational dances in other ballets, for example in those for the tradespeople in Ashton's *Cinderella*.

To some extent the heroes and heroines of classical ballet also use occupational gesture when they indicate horse riding, hunting, lute-playing and singing. But by and large these are only examples of the gesture as an item on its own, MacMillan is one of

Les Patineurs   Ballets with a theme – Ashton's view of skaters. 'All go together' (The Royal Ballet)

the rare choreographers who has used occupational gesture as an integral part of the dance. For example, in *Romeo and Juliet* this aspect of his choreography is seen at its finest in the *pas de trois* for Romeo, Mercutio and Benvolio before they enter the Capulet ball. They ride, fence and parry with swords, and sing a song with a lute. The gestures they make are at one with their interesting footwork. The footwork appears again and again in different *enchaînements* during their other appearances, notably in the short solo for Mercutio when he dances in a more tragic vein just before he dies.

Ashton, too, has made vivid use of occupational gesture from time to time as, for example, when his 'Swiss Miss' milks her cow with the help of the three boys in *Façade*. One of his finest examples of occupational gesture as the foundation of a ballet remains *Les Patineurs*. Here he creates the many happy and not so happy incidents that can occur on a skating rink where even a professional can 'miss a trick'.

Jerome Robbins has a knack of using occupational gesture in many of his works and most particularly in *The Concert*, where the well-observed behaviour of the many different concert-goers arouses much laughter. Those in the audience who have had to suffer such behaviour in a concert hall, whilst trying to listen to a brilliant musician, know that his remarks about certain characters are only too true.

Whatever occupational gesture (mime) a choreographer chooses to use in ballet, it must be envisaged in terms of dance without the use of props. Even such mundane tasks as eating or drinking have found a place in some ballets. Because on the stage they acquire importance, they must be seen to have a proper purpose. This is usually to throw light on the character being played or to create the right atmosphere for the location of the action and for the expressive action required for the unfolding of the plot or theme.

The Concert   Robbins' view of concert-goers. The Listeners (The Royal Ballet)

The romantic style

The romantic style is the most poetic of all because its movements must express moods, emotions and actions that are reactions to the circumstances and events which surround and occur to characters during the unfolding of plot, theme or music.

There are two kinds of romantic ballet. Firstly, there are ballets of the older type which depict the struggle between the world of the flesh and the world of the spirit and which were usually inspired by a fairy tale or legend, e.g. *La Sylphide* and *Giselle*. Secondly, there are modern works which are based on tales of passionate love, often frustrated or unrequited, and usually ending in tragedy, e.g. *Romeo and Juliet*, *A Month in the Country* and *The Invitation*.

The two kinds of romantic ballet

A The first kind developed out of the Romantic movement which emerged at a time when artists of all kinds rebelled against being servants in wealthy households, obeying their patrons' orders and being regulated by religious, political and other advisers. They broke away to work independently and become their own masters. Inspired by Dante's *Divine Comedy* and the sad tale of his love for Beatrice and by medieval ballads about a knight saving a damsel in distress, their works told of lovers in search of a beloved, a metaphor for the 'artist in search of his muse'. But the beloved was unattainable either because she belonged to another or because, like his muse, she forever eluded him as she was only a figment of his imagination. Such romantic stories and ballads inspired many nineteenth-century ballets, directly or indirectly, from Petipa's *Raymonda*, Massine's *Symphonie Fantastique* and Lenau's *Don Juan* (to the tone poem by Strauss which was later to inspire an Ashton ballet) to *La Sonnambula* (Balanchine's ballet based on Bellini's opera which was based on a Walter Scott novel, see page 33).

Such plots gave choreographers scope to stage dances in which the world of the flesh could be exemplified by folk style or *demi-caractère* dances and that of the world of the spirit with the newly developed 'flight *sur les pointes*' and softly lyrical *ports de bras* which epitomised the heroine's ethereal being. This style allowed other-worldly figures to express themselves more naturally than in classical ballet where technical precision and command over conventional gesture were necessary. Such romantic libretti required a choreographer to have a greater understanding of the significance of each movement, particularly if the protagonists came from different classes or environments as in *La Sylphide* (a farmer and a fairy) or *Giselle* (a count and a peasant).

Fokine's advice to those wishing to create the romantic style of dance was much as for *demi-caractère* when he said: 'The choreographer should base his design on classical technique from the feet to the waist, but above that the dancer's head, body and arms must be free to express the moods, emotions and actions of the character in the story or theme to be communicated.' This style was first created by Taglioni for his daughter Marie. The tale of *La Sylphide* gave him an opportunity to exploit her expressive arms and face as well as her ability to dance *sur les pointes*. Perrot developed the style in his dances for Carlotta Grisi in *Giselle*. It was then expanded by Fokine and used in both grave and gay moods in *Les Sylphides* and *Le Carnaval*, where it is particularly expressive of both meaning and music. In both ballets he incorporated several conventional gestures in the *ports de bras* but also demanded

Les Sylphides   Fokine's interpretation of romantic ballet
'Let the music tell you what to do' (The Royal Ballet)

greater emotional involvement from the dancers. These changes added to the overall meaning communicated by the dancing. He used to say: 'Listen to the music, let it tell you what to do.'

The above ballets are classified under the nineteenth-century meaning of the term 'romantic' because they are based in the world of fantasy and deal very subtly with the theme of Man's struggle against fate. When Fokine was asked who was the male figure in *Les Sylphides* he replied: 'Perhaps he is Love himself in a romantic, nostalgic mood. I do not know. I made it for a dancer (Nijinsky) who can soar like a spirit, but who has the strength to dance with the Wilis [as in *Giselle*] and live to dance again.' When talking about *Le Carnaval*, he added: 'Pierrot was the strange tragic clown known all over Europe as the little man – he who gets slapped. He is the odd man out at the ball, he only wants one kiss, but it always eludes him.' The theme of the 'little man' made and still makes Fokine's *Petrushka* so memorable.

Petrushka   Fokine's second Russian ballet
Petrushka's cry – 'He who gets slapped' (David Bintley)

Ashton's re-working of the old story of *Ondine* (with music by Hans Werner Henze) was a perfect modern version of the older type of romantic ballet. He not only used very expressive *ports de bras* for his other-worldly characters but changed the usual conception of classical pointe-work. Ondine, the sea nymph (Margot Fonteyn) so used her feet that she appeared always to float through water. This was done by a series of *pas marchés* each of which softly rose and fell through her feet from toe to heel. They were co-ordinated with a soft undulating movement of the arms. Ashton thus created a special style for a particular character which summed up – as it were – her whole being, but which would have been unsuitable for any other ballet.

B Once Fokine had demonstrated that mimed dance and danced mime were the best materials to use in ballets where individual characters had to stand out from the rest of the cast, and particularly when true love did not run smoothly, other choreographers followed suit. Although in some ways twentieth-century romantic ballets resemble those of the nineteenth century, they more often originate in a drama which supposedly takes place in the world of reality. Moreover they nearly always end in tragedy because the protagonists reach out in some way for the unattainable.

The events and circumstances surrounding such plots are difficult to control and organise because the characters are supposedly living in the real world. So the choreographer cannot make strong contrasts between the style usually used for the other-worldly spirits and that used for the characters living in the particular setting. He can only highlight the atmosphere supporting the plot, especially those circumstances where he has to portray differences between classes and thus general behaviour, idiosyncrasies, etc., for example the contrast that must be made between the dances for all and sundry in the town square and those for the aristocrats in the ballroom of *Romeo and Juliet*. Nevertheless every choreographer creating this kind of romantic ballet today has to spend much time creating the proper gestures to replace the words, which in such ballets are never spoken but must be understood. If the dancers perform those gestures with feeling and understanding they will express the moods, emotions and actions of the characters they play. This is what happens in MacMillan's *Romeo and Juliet* and Ashton's *A Month in the Country*.

It is perhaps appropriate to stress again that where playwrights require pages of dialogue to explain every factor in the development of the plot, to create a changing atmosphere and to show how the actions affect the actors in the play, dancers can communicate whole passages of dialogue in a few expressive gestures woven into *enchaînements*. (As played by the Moscow Arts Theatre, Turgenev's *A Month in the Country* takes over two hours, Ashton's ballet roughly half an hour.) Only characters and episodes essential to the plot are retained. All others can be eliminated because they are there to create atmosphere, which in ballet can be supplied by the music, set and appropriate costumes. MacMillan and Ashton understood this and emphasised the main action. Their work should be studied by all would-be choreographers.

The development of the individual character

Unlike classical or *demi-caractère* ballets today's romantic ballets have few stereotyped heroes and heroines because they deal with the moods, emotions and actions of one or more individuals in response to their circumstances and the unfolding of the plot. Their movements must, therefore, have literal implications even though they use the flowing romantic style originated by Taglioni and Perrot in *La Sylphide* and *Giselle*. What is meant by the term 'literal'?

> *Literal:* 'taking words in their usual and primary sense and applying the ordinary rules of grammar without mysticism, allegory or metaphor' (O.E.D.)

A choreographer should translate this definition into dance terms thus: taking the moods, emotions and actions expressed, understood and observed by everyone in general and using natural gestures when applying the rules of choreographic grammar without trying to express them in any other way. Twentieth-century choreographers rarely deal with fairyland; they prefer to depict real characters living in a particular environment who have strong individual traits. They must take a realistic view and look objectively when deciding which movements will best describe individuality. No better example of such objectivity was Ashton's own playing of the Onlooker in *Nocturne*. He stood silent and still, watching the tragedy of the Poor Girl who was being rejected by the Rich Man. His two tiny gestures said everything and expressed the audience's understanding of the plot. He made one as if he should try and comfort her, but turned away, walked upstage and on the balcony with his back to the audience, raised his arms widely only to drop them helplessly. No one could fail to understand the Onlooker's reaction to the tale just unfolded. To some extent the same idea of an onlooker applies to that of Jaeger, the critic in *Enigma Variations*. He is there as the only one who fully understands the problems of both Elgar and his Wife, but plays no part in the other activities. And, although Bratfisch in MacMillan's *Mayerling* is a dancing role, he, too, is an onlooker who only shows his real self during his final entrance and last gesture as he throws his flower into Mary Vetsera's grave.

However hard modern choreographers may try there are bound to be similarities to older ballets because their vocabulary is not limitless. Nor are the dancers' physical abilities. Certain steps, poses and gestures are bound to recur because tradition has demonstrated time and again that technically there are certain sure ways of giving the design dimension, variety and texture. These ways have become so much a part of the fabric of dance that they are used almost unknowingly by teachers and dancers. Ashton and MacMillan do show that changes can be made. To take only one example, their use of the *arabesque* as a gesture. Its style of performance and expression change repeatedly throughout each ballet as the dancer changes with the attendant circumstances. The *arabesque* as a gesture changes to give some insight into the character's moods, emotions and actions, as well as arising out of the rhythmic and melodic phrasing of the music.

There is an obvious contrast in Ashton's *Enigma Variations* between the youthful Dorabella's playful and loving *arabesques* in front of Elgar and the *arabesques* of his Wife, which are calm and tenderly sympathetic when she dances with him. Another vivid contrast can be seen in MacMillan's *The Invitation*. When the Young Girl first dances with her Cousin her *arabesques* are tentative but outward-going. When she meets him after her seduction by the Older Man, they are tragically tense and withdrawn. She is too afraid, even ashamed, to move towards her Cousin even though he is gentle and understanding in his wish to comfort her. He has learnt his lesson through being seduced by the Older Woman.

The above examples demonstrate what can be done if a ballet is to communicate meaning beyond that of distinguishing between the world of the flesh and that of the spirit. Another firm distinction which both Ashton and MacMillan make clear is

A Month in the Country   Ashton's romantic style
Natalia and the Tutor embrace for the first time (Lynn Seymour, Anthony Dowell)

between the dances of youth and age or innocence and experience. Dorabella's lively personality with its carefree lack of attention to technical details is in contrast to Mrs Elgar's more disciplined, thoughtful movements. Another side of youthfulness is exploited in *Enigma Variations*, that of awakening love. The episode of the 'enchanting Isobel Fitton' being swung in her hammock by and then dancing with Richard Arnold. They both display a new awareness of each other and this colours their movements. She is a little playful, first accepting and then rejecting his advances, whilst he suggests there are stronger feelings behind his efforts to steal a kiss. Such feelings are also suggested when the Cousin first meets the Young Girl in *The Invitation*. The Young Girl's movements are innocent and child-like unlike those of Isobel and the shock of seduction makes a far greater impact on her whole being. This is shown vividly when, left finally alone, she strikes a dramatic pose of complete withdrawal from love and happiness.

Dorabella's playfulness is similar to that of Natalia's ward, Vera, when she first dances in *A Month in the Country*. The carefree quality disappears when she shyly tries to tell the Tutor how fond she has become of him, and when she discovers Natalia and the Tutor in each other's arms, she loses all inhibitions to denounce them. Her shy confession of love is in deep contrast to that of Natalia, who cannot wait to show that her emotions are fully aroused when left alone with the same man. It is in these brief intimate scenes that Ashton exploits the difference between youth falling in love and experience demanding it, because Natalia is used to getting her own way.

It may be asked: 'How does the Tutor react to these situations?' Ashton's choreography follows the style used by the Moscow Arts Theatre production of the play – he is danced in the ballet in the same way as he is acted in Russia. The Tutor is a student of peasant origin who has taken a job teaching the son of a wealthy merchant whose household is spending the summer in their country dacha. In Ashton's version, as in the Russian staged version, the Tutor's encounter with Katia, the servant girl, allows him momentarily to be back home amongst his master's peasants. So he relaxes and enjoys a brief dance with her after she has fed him with cherries. Later he responds more positively to Vera's shy advances and embraces her gently but respectfully when they are interrupted by Natalia. The latter's vicious slap on the child's face explains more than any other gesture Natalia's selfishness. Yet the Tutor's capitulation to Natalia reveals her power over every man she meets as well as his failure to withstand her wiles. Ashton's careful build-up to this climax makes Vera's discovery of them in each other's arms all the more poignant because she shows a child-like petulance at losing one she so longed to have for her own. It is so unlike Natalia's reaction when finding the Tutor and Vera together. The Tutor remains a sympathetic character for Vera's sorrow at his departure is echoed by Kolia, Natalia's son, when he too realises he is losing the only person who has tried to make him happy.

If would-be choreographers examine Ashton's *The Dream* they will discover the significant development that has been made in the structure of the old kind of romantic ballet. Certainly Ashton makes a clear distinction between the dances of the Fairies and those of the Mechanicals. The dances of the Four Lovers belong to both worlds. The Fairies giggle at their antics as they do at those of Bottom and their Queen. 'Lord, what fools we mortals be', are Shakespeare's own words and it is this particular comment that Ashton has used as the keynote to the adventures in the forest.

Another aspect of Ashton's design are the strong individual traits shown by all the leading characters. Despite the contrast he makes between the dances of Puck and

The Dream Ashton's interpretation of Shakespeare: Titania 'lighter than air' (Antoinette Sibley) . . .

... Puck – 'Lord what fools' (Simon Rice)

Bottom, between those of the Lovers in the *pas de deux* and those of Titania and Bottom, the movements grow out of a firm technical choreographic design. Ashton looks back to Petipa's more formal style because it is suitable for Mendelssohn's music. Despite Puck's wild leaps, crazy antics and turns, the clumsy attempts by the Mechanicals to 'cut capers' and Bottom's efforts *sur les pointes*, it is Oberon and Titania's dancing that commands the stage as well as those trapped in the 'magicked' Athenian wood. From their first confrontation, when Titania appears wilfully aloof as Oberon tries to exert his authority, to their final reconciliation, they stand out as a true Fairy King and Queen, who are not beyond suffering the moods and emotions of 'We mortals here'.

Technical characteristics

If choreographers study the above works of Ashton and MacMillan, they will understand how far the art of choreography has developed since Fokine changed its structure and texture. They will perhaps understand even better if they pay particular attention to the fine details of every movement. It is no longer the case that the romantic style means dancing classically from the feet to the waist and above that allowing the body, arms and head to express themselves to describe the moods, emotions and actions of the characters.

113

It is well known that only a great dancer-artist can suggest the development of the sixteen-year-old Aurora, happy at her birthday, into the dreamy figure the Prince meets in the woodland glade and on to her final entrance as a triumphant Princess fully awake to her responsibilities as Queen-to-be. The *enchaînements* she dances thoughout the three scenes do not change in style or content. When Diaghilev staged *The Sleeping Beauty* in London (1921) two of his Auroras were princesses by marriage and ballerinas assolutas by Imperial decree. They were grand princesses dancing superbly throughout, but never once suggested that they grew from girl to woman by any change of expression or ways of dancing. Yet if the dances of Vera and Natalia in *A Month in the Country* and Juliet in *Romeo and Juliet* are examined it will be discovered how the technical content is so designed that the steps, poses and gestures show how changing circumstances are affecting the individuals. This is what Perrot first attempted with his five leitmotifs for *Giselle* (see page 61).

Continual development in the choreographic design is very obvious in the quiver of the raised leg as the Tutor takes Natalia in his arms. It shows her growing emotional involvement and gradually seems to affect her every movement. This same tiny movement also appears when Vera begins to dance with the Tutor, but her movement is not so intense. It does not develop into the passionate circling *en l'air* that occurs when the Tutor swings Natalia round as she rests on his knee before they ultimately turn to face each other and embrace. This particularly subtle quiver of the leg to express newly aroused emotion was first noticed in Ashton's *The Two Pigeons* when the Young Girl and her friends pretend to strut around like pigeons. But when she repeats the movement in her dance with the Young Man, it appears in a different context, that of awakening love. When he leaves her for the Gipsy and she dances

The Two Pigeons   Ashton's delicate use of movement: the wanderer returns . . .

. . . the quivering foot (Lynn Seymour, David Wall)

alone, it becomes a sad reflection of what has been. When the Young Man returns and the movement is again repeated more slowly and deliberately it becomes the signal of a tender reunion.

Somewhat similar changes take place in MacMillan's dances for Juliet. His ever-developing design gives the vital clues to Juliet's development from a child playing with her doll to the shy recipient of Paris' respectful admiration. Juliet then becomes the slightly apprehensive debutante at the Ball where her movements, though tentative, are conventionally correct when she dances with Paris. The moment she encounters Romeo and senses somehow that her life has changed her movement becomes more purposeful. From there onwards it becomes stronger and more emotional so that her joyous movements and later abandon in Romeo's arms are in absolute contrast to her later dance with Paris. Her movements then are equally purposeful but they are constricted and withdrawn, so that her Father's contemptuous rejection of her pleas and his throwing her to the floor seem the proper outcome of what in his eyes is sheer disobedience. It is her final passionate abandon on discovering Romeo's body that demonstrates how overwhelming sorrow can destroy all sense of discipline over both body and mind.

Romeo and Juliet MacMillan's interpretation of Shakespeare
Left: Romeo and Juliet's first meeting at the ball; above: 'My heart's dear Love' – Balcony scene (Lesley Collier, Wayne Eagling)

Although *Mayerling* is not itself a romantic ballet, it is involved with love affairs. In the deterioration of Count Rudolf's manners and behaviour, MacMillan shows more clearly than anywhere else in his works how any mental and physical breakdown must show through and beyond the technicalities of the dance. The portrayal of this tragic figure is possibly one of the most demanding of all male roles because of the sheer complexity of the incidents where Rudolf is always the centre. Everything focuses on the fact that he is always struggling with his desire for love and power as well as for an end to all his problems. In no way is he shown in a sympathetic light. Nor can one feel any sympathy for the various ladies in his life, all of whom conform outwardly to the strict etiquette of the enclosed society of the Austrian court. Yet they are all prepared to intrigue one with another to gain more power over the tragic Count. Even Mary Vetsera has only one wish, to be possessed by him, and is prepared to go to any lengths to achieve that end. It is possible to say that their *pas de deux* are completely uninhibited. Here, there is no tenderness, no lyricism, only sheer brutal passion in which technical discipline is seemingly thrown to the winds. Not one of Rudolf's other ladies has been so embraced. Nor has any of them had to respond so intensely to his wishes. Yet the discipline of MacMillan's design in all its variety, dimension and structure requires each dancer to understand and conform to technical discipline. It is this which makes the performance capable of repetition. A comparison of Rudolf's apparently undisciplined emotions with the subtle feelings expressed by Bratfisch, his valet, shows how MacMillan creates some relief even within the decadence and horror.

Natural emotional expression

Because the characters of *A Month in the Country*, *Enigma Variations*, *Romeo and Juliet*, *The Invitation* and *Mayerling* are supposedly living in a real world, the choreographers have no need to make many deliberate contrasts in the style of dance. Certainly there is a difference between classes when, for example, the Tutor dances first with Katia the servant, and then with Natalia in *A Month in the Country* or when townspeople dance in the street and nobles in the ballroom in *Romeo and Juliet*. Nevertheless much more attention has to be given to the *ports de bras* of all types of character in such ballets because these supply the words not spoken in dance. If the *ports de bras* are to be convincing, choreographers need to study Natural Emotional Expression. In the same way as conventional gesture (see page 88), it has its rules which were formulated by John Davies in 'Orchestra, A Poem of Dancing' (1594). In it he discusses 'the Motions seven that are in Nature found' (Stanza 73). These rules give the directions into which the head, body and arms should move when expressing certain moods, emotions and actions.

1 Upwards and outwards The head, body and arms rise upwards and outwards in all the happy emotions as can be seen in the final dances of *The Sleeping Beauty*, *La Fille Mal Gardée* and *Daphnis and Chloë*.

If the movement only goes upwards it usually means pride or arrogance.

2 Downwards and inwards The head, body and arms move downwards and inwards in all the sad emotions as in the final dance of the Swans in *Swan Lake* and the opening dance of *Requiem*.

If the movement is only downwards it usually means disgrace or tiredness.

118

3 Sideways open (*écarté* or *effacé*) The head, body and arms open out boldly in such a way that the performer is seen to be fully revealed to all as an honest, sincere person who has no need to dissemble. The movements are more or less directed sideways, i.e. *écarté* or *effacé*, as in the dances for Romeo, Mercutio and Benvolio in *Romeo and Juliet* and for the Tutor in *A Month in the Country*.

4 Sideways closed (*croisé*) If the character moves sideways with the head, body and arms in some way averted from the front, i.e. *croisé*, possibly with a twist of the shoulders, he or she is usually playing some evil or cunning person. One of the finest examples used to be de Valois' dance for the Three Comforters in *Job*. Their twisted cunning movements were vividly contrasted with those she created for Elihu, the personification of Youth and Truth. The best present-day example of the cunning gestures are those of Rudolf's Four Friends, the conspirators in *Mayerling*.

5 Forwards A dancer coming forwards can convey a variety of meaning: giving a greeting; asking a question, even if it is only an inquisitive movement of the head; saying Yes, or agreeing with a nod or with a particular wave of the hand; giving something with arms circling outwards, e.g. Natalia and the Tutor when they open their arms to each other; or merely proffering a hand at the beginning of a dance, e.g. Paris offering his hand to Juliet.

6 Backwards There is a backwards movement in saying No, which can be a slight withdrawal of head and shoulders; a more emphatic shake of the head perhaps accompanied by the hand pushing away an undesirable request or person, e.g. Juliet's rejection of Paris in the Bedroom scene. More importantly, there is always a withdrawal backwards or turn aside in moments of fear. This movement is usually made more apparent because the head sinks into the shoulders and the hands come close to the body to protect it from some blow, curse or frightening event, e.g. Juliet's movement after her father has demanded why she is not conforming to his wishes.

7 The turn The seventh direction is a 'Turn around' which John Davies suggests is like a stop in some sentence or dance. The conversation is ended or the speaker has changed his or her mind. There are many uses for this turn, particularly when dancers are conversing in *ports de bras*. One of the most beautiful is probably that of Odette in the Act II *pas de deux* of *Swan Lake* when, overcoming her fear at being captured, she turns her head and deliberately looks into Siegfried's eyes.

A study of how people react in real life when affected by any kind of emotion and mood soon reveals how the movements of the whole body can change. Sometimes they are perceived only by those in intimate contact, yet sometimes they can make everyone in a large crowd aware of individual feelings. The choreographer's problem is how to make subtle or vigorous gesture visible to those on the other side of the footlights. Success will depend very largely on the dancer's own sense of timing and ability so to perform the gestures created that they convey meaning which makes sense within the context of the ballet. This can be done only if the whole body is seen to be involved in some way or other. It also depends on how the gesture is extended in time and space so that it appears to emanate from the dancer's concentration on the purpose of the gesture. Amongst the greatest dancer-mimes even the slightest wink becomes obvious. De Valois, Ashton and MacMillan have studied paintings and drawings by English artists and/or the words of such great playwrights as Shakespeare and translated them into gestures for which the dancer's whole body has to play a part.

Character and National styles

Character and/or National styles of ballet can be linked in some ways to that of *demi-caractère*. Character dance like *demi-caractère* dance had its beginnings in *La Fille Mal Gardée* when farmers and peasants were first allowed to set foot on the Royal and Imperial stages, which had hitherto been the home of gods and goddesses or noble and well-born heroes and heroines. But as Napoleon's initial conquests and later defeats made European countries aware of their own traditional arts, so choreographers, like composers, authors, poets and painters, began to strengthen the national features of their work. More typical and traditional folk dance steps and customs were absorbed into *demi-caractère* dance and were accompanied by idiomatic features from national music. When this happened, however, even the traditional features became more stereotyped because choreographers used only those which the audience could easily recognise and which were commonly seen and heard in a particular country.

It was from such traditional dance that Fokine, at the instigation of Diaghilev, devised the first truly national ballets by breaking away from the sterotyped steps. Instead, Fokine based his design (as did the composer Stravinsky and the artist Korovin (later Goncharova)) on the folk tales, customs, traditional dances and music of Russia without in any way conforming to the generally accepted rules of classical technique. *The Firebird* set the example for many nationally styled ballets such as *Petrushka*, *The Rake's Progress* and *Rodeo*. These are seen to belong to one particular country and are at their best when performed by dancers from that country.

Definition of Character and National ballet

A *Character Ballet* is one in which classical technique is discarded except where it is used to depict particular and usually fantastic characters as for the dolls in *Petrushka* and *La Boutique Fantasque*. Instead, a particular style of dance is used through which the performers play strongly defined characters who express not only social status in a particular community but also moods, emotions and actions, which are alien to the calm spaciousness of classical dance. Such ballets range from *The Green Table* (Kurt Jooss 1933) and *Façade* (Ashton 1931) to Robbins' *Fancy Free* (1944).

A *National Ballet* is one which is based firstly on the traditional stories, dance, music and customs of a particular country and/or secondly on the atmosphere, texture and typical life of a country. Examples of such ballets are Fokine's *The Firebird* and *Petrushka*, de Valois' *Job* and *The Rake's Progress* and Ashton's *La Fille Mal Gardée*, the last of which, despite its French origin, discloses the particular quality of English theatre customs and comedy, as does Cranko's *Pineapple Poll*. The Americans have such ballets as Loring's *Billy the Kid* and De Mille's *Rodeo* and *Fall River Legend*. The Russians have their twelve ballets based on Pushkin's poems such as *The Fountain of Bakhchisarai* and the Czechs have *The Gingerbread Heart*. In fact most countries have chosen to reflect something of their own heritage.

David Bintley's *Hobson's Choice* (1989) is in the same category as *The Rake's Progress*. Like Hogarth, Harold Brighouse, the author of the play, discussed the problems and topics current in Salford in the early nineteen twenties such as class barriers, women's rights, temperance, pubs and music-hall jokes. Bintley's rumbustious choreography reflects all these through a rich mixture of social, clog, stage and traditional dance, which are richly echoed by Paul Reade's evocative score. The cast enter into this Lancashire hot-pot as to the manner born and only a snob will fail to enjoy: 'By gum! What a Ballet' daring to show itself in the Opera House.

Nineteenth-century choreographers creating either a character or a national ballet used both occupational and natural emotional gesture in their dance designs. They had to be more specific about the traditionally accepted forms of behaviour, customs, occupations and particular national characteristics. It was the impact of the Polovtsian Warriors and their dances from *Prince Igor* (1910) that startled Parisian and other audiences into recognition that even the most barbaric dance had a rightful place in the theatre.

The differences between character dance and dances of character

A distinction must be made between character dance and dances of character. It was first made by Dauberval when staging *La Fille Mal Gardée*. He described the former as derived from traditional sources and given theatrical form which demonstrated how his peasants and farmers would move in everyday life. The latter he created specially to depict Alain, a very particular role which was unlikely to appear in any other ballet.

A distinction should also be made between the particular style of character dance known in all the leading schools and the true folk dance performed by the people of a country. The former was derived from traditional sources but stylised by Saint-Léon, who gave much thought to the theatrical presentation of such material. This development of a character style happened after Napoleon's campaigns which gave birth to the so-called National movements. These led such Russian composers as Glinka and those known as 'The Mighty Little Heap' to create operas and tone poems on traditional stories, and Pushkin and Lermontov to write poems in the language spoken by the Russian people. Later, what is now known as National music was composed by such musicians as the Czechs Smetana and Dvorak, the Hungarian Liszt, the Norwegian Grieg, the Spanish Granados, Albeniz and De Falla, the Polish Chopin and, finally, the English Elgar and Vaughan-Williams.

Rules for staging character dance

Saint-Léon laid down certain rules for the staging of character dance based on the traditional folk dance of a particular country. These rules are still of value and are widely followed throughout Europe and Asia.

1 Steps should be classified under the terms used in the classical vocabulary so that they have a commonly recognised form, e.g. the three changes of weight required by the Russian 'Kolokol' or bell step and the Hungarian 'Harang' make them *pas de bourrée*, whilst the 'goat's leap' known in several countries becomes the *pas de chat*.

2 Emphasis must be placed on certain steps and their qualities which appear to be particular to one country and dances should be limited to those which can be recognised. The movements of Hungarian dance are 'down to the earth' whereas those of Scottish Highland dance are 'away from the earth'.

3 In order to display particular native features, the traditional circle, chain and couple dance formations must be broken up and opened outwards so that the steps are seen clearly by the audience. This is after all what the first balletmasters did when professionals appeared on stage and were no longer surrounded by the court where all eyes were focused on the king (see page 76).

4 The very particular relationship of the accenting and phrasing of the steps with the overall and short phrase rhythms and accents of the music must be maintained.

It was shortly after Saint-Léon's arrival in Russia that he instigated the teaching of the so-called character dance at the Imperial St. Petersburg Theatrical Academy. In thoroughly systematised form it now applies throughout the USSR. Much of the syllabus has become part of the training of dancers all over the world. Its features are very much the same as those described earlier in connection with *demi-caractère* style (see page 93) but with a very strong difference. The steps are always performed in boots or heeled shoes so all the movements look stronger and often heavier. They require accurate timing and neat footwork if the accents are to be heard and seen. The *ports de bras* must be more emphatic and be accurately placed.

The partnership between boy and girl must be carefully observed and timed because each country has its own forms for such joint movement.

Hungarian The couples frequently face each other looking into each other's faces and appear to crouch over their feet slightly which emphasises the 'down to earth' quality as most steps appear to go down into and not out of the ground. (See page 95 for other characteristics.)

Polish The boy's way of appearing to guide his girl just in front of him in all travelling steps affects the carrige of both himself and his partner. The constant use of what is called the 'feminine cadence' is a particular rhythmic feature. This is when a phrase finishes on the second (or weak) and not on the first or third beat of a final bar. It is usually accompanied by a firm clipping of the heels together and is noticeable in all mazurkas and polonaises, particularly in the steps that Saint-Léon called the *promenade*, *cabriole* and *pas sissonne* (see page 121).

Spanish In all Spanish Theatre dances there must be strict control over the stance taken. Bodies should be fully stretched upwards and curved either slightly forwards or backwards from the waist only. This stance must be accompanied by the well-recognised *ports de bras*, which must be accurately co-ordinated with the footwork. The arms usually change after each brief *enchaînement*. Their movement also depends upon which foot is in front. If the right foot remains there for several bars, the arms will be held still, but as soon as the left moves in front the arms will change. There is also a tendency to pause in a pose at the end of a phrase and for a deliberate change to be made before further dance.

An interesting point to note in real Spanish folk dance is that the boy and girl rarely touch each other. In some older dances they each hold a corner of a handkerchief to form a link and in some areas they link little fingers.

Italian There is little to distinguish between the Italian character dance and its *demi-caractère* form save only that heeled shoes are worn and thus from time to time take on a slightly Spanish flavour, the only difference perhaps being the more fluid way of phrasing and less rigidly accurate timing of the steps.

For all their liveliness of style any of the above national dances seen in one ballet resemble those in another because choreographers such as Petipa, Bournonville and Saint-Léon utilised the same steps and *ports de bras* again and again. Only the music created slight differences and this not markedly because the composers used the best of commonly recognised traditional musical idioms. Possibly the best of commonly recognised character dance styles are found in *Coppélia*, *Swan Lake* (Old and Soviet versions) and *La Boutique Fantasque*. Even Massine's choreographic genius realised that the old stylised forms were the best way to portray the national dolls sold in the shop. It is, however, easy to recognise that the choreography for *The Three-Cornered Hat* has greater authenticity because it is based on the folk and flamenco dance Massine had studied in Spain. He made his design choreographically viable by distinguishing clearly between the two styles he was using. By so differentiating he described both the characteristics of his villagers and the typical gestures which enabled them to tell their tale (see page 59).

Massine's brilliant use of descriptive and narrative gestures in *The Three-Cornered Hat* was a proper development of Fokine's mimed dance and danced mime, first seen in *The Firebird* and *Petrushka*. As already noted, the dances Fokine staged for the nursemaids, coachmen and others at the Fair were 'real dances' (see page 59). They created the atmosphere and mood, but the narrative was told by the dolls using specially created movements which could be called dances of character.

Characters from the commedia dell'arte

When Dauberval defined what he meant by dances of character he undoubtedly had in mind some easily recognised characters of the commedia dell'arte, whose actors regularly played such roles as the absent-minded doctor or scientist, miser, termagant wife or widow and various clowns such as the sad Pierrot or zany clown. He was aware that famous players of those roles had developed their own ways of interpretation and tricks, which were then handed down from generation to generation. Some part of their play still exists. For example: Mother Simone in Pavlova's version of *La Fille Mal Gardée* which I saw in Kiev (1954) was played by a man and used such tricks as titivating before meeting Father Thomas and fainting when Lise is discovered in her bedroom with Colas. Alain was played as an idiot who hardly danced at all except to fall over his own feet. In fact they were stereotypes, well known in the popular theatre and instantly recognised as are supercilious members of the upper classes, superior servants and prostitutes. This is useful when telling a story, particularly as prostitutes appear in many ballets. One expects and sees silk stockings or nowadays fish-net tights on made-up hussies with split or very short skirts, or brief frilly knickers, low-necked bodices or tight gaudy corsets, elaborate hair-dos or hats, and so on. They are found in ballets by Jooss, Massine, MacMillan and others. Yet in *The Rake's Progress* de Valois found something new to say about the ladies of the town when she made their leader kick off her shoes, pull up her long yellow skirt and roll down her red stockings before bursting barefooted into a riotous dance on a great salver. Other ladies of doubtful

The Rake's Progress English National Ballet and de Valois' interpretation of Hogarth's evils of the day
The Prostitute and the Rake (June Highwood, Desmond Kelly)

virtue take similar liberties when they drop their skirts, as happens in Ashton's Polka in
Façade. But MacMillan's street dancers and cabaret girls in *Mayerling* are stereotypes.

There are very different ways of presenting these old characters even whilst
preserving their basic form. From the beginning of his career Ashton frequently used
the old stereotypes but created unique dances which can be called a translation of
favourite comic play into the language of ballet. Foremost amongst the dances are
those for Bottom, in *The Dream*, when he is transformed into an ass. Here is the clown
whose clumsy, naïve behaviour is exemplified by his 'tottering *sur les pointes*',
scratching his back on a bush and performing other antics when he dances with
Titania. How moving are his gestures when, once again himself, he muses: 'Methought
I was, I know not what methought.' Ashton enlarged this choreographic gem in *The
Tales of Beatrix Potter* when Pigling Bland and the Black Berkshire indulge in a
delicate *pas de deux*, both *sur les pointes*. Ashton's Mother Simone in *La Fille Mal
Gardée* is rightly played by a man who adopts stereotyped female behaviour, but gone
is the non-dancing character of the older versions. This Simone has come directly from
playing the Dame of pantomime and maintains that character from her very first
entrance when she shakes a tablecloth out of the window and then furiously throws

every vegetable in sight at Colas because she finds him waiting for Lise. But – of course – being of a frugal mind, saving the pot before finally flinging the geranium. She later shows her mettle as a clog dancer abetted by four pretty girls, tries to set her cap at Father Thomas, but finally realises she cannot frustrate true love and dances out happily with the rest.

This English pantomime tradition Ashton also exploited earlier in his choreography for the Ugly Sisters in *Cinderella* where he followed the tradition that one is always a somewhat modest violet bossed about by her dragon of a sister. This double characterisation was made more hilarious at the first performances when the bossy one was danced by Helpmann, and later the taller MacMillan, with wonderfully extended *développés*, and the shyer one by Ashton with dainty attempts to be correct at all costs. A similar incongruous matching of the very tall girl with one of the shortest boys in MacMillan's *Elite Syncopations* reveals that he, too, understands that old music-hall and pantomime practices are a wonderful source of inspiration if a British audience is to laugh and enjoy the occasion as the dancers do.

Another commedia dell'arte character whose play has influenced too few choreographers is that of Harlequin, a maker of mischief, a 'magicker of spells', an animal impersonator and always a great dancer. Fokine's Harlequin only gives a glimpse of his abilities. Ashton's Puck in *The Dream* uses all his 'bag of tricks' as envisaged by Shakespeare. The whole performance is based on the classical vocabulary of steps shorn of every convention so that he can go 'swifter than an arrow from an archer's bow'. Every leap, turn, beat and somersault is perfectly co-ordinated with the phrase and with the music despite the fact that the dance scarcely reflects the period when the music was composed as does Ashton's choreography in other ballets (see page 42). Choreographers should therefore note that it is possible to design movements which may contradict the music that is being played, but not if they contradict the mood and rhythmic qualities of the whole context. Mendelssohn's music is light-hearted. It does not probe the deeper emotions. Nor is it any more than the incidental music to a play that captured the composer's imagination and inspired him to conjure up the 'goings on in the Magicked Athenian wood'. Thus in his own way Ashton has reflected the composer's own imaginative flight of fancy, firstly by following the academic structure of the score and secondly by using his choreographic imagination to bring to life Shakespeare's mortals and immortals for 'of such stuff dreams are made'.

Another source for dances of character can be found in the sad clown or 'the man who gets slapped'. They range variously from Fokine's Pierrot in *Le Carnaval* who only wants 'one kiss' and his puppet *Petrushka* who wants to be free to Ashton's Alain mentioned above and MacMillan's Bratfisch in *Mayerling*. Such a lonely figure is always pathetic because whatever he wants proves impossible to have. Only in *Petrushka* is he seen to be the principal player in the action and even then only the actor-dancer's complete commitment to the whole and complete loyalty to Fokine's design make him dominate the action. As yet there has been no other attempt to describe so vividly in dance the wish of any character, but in this case a puppet, to escape from prison. MacMillan's Bratfisch tries to keep his employer amused and thus to postpone the inevitable tragedy. He only reveals his true feelings when he throws his flower into Mary Vetsera's grave just before the curtain falls. His dance throughout has its base in the classical vocabulary but MacMillan has coloured it by gestures from cabaret and vaudeville dance traditions, which serve to reveal not only class differences in behaviour but also genuine feelings. This is why Bratfisch is so important. Without him there is no other character with whom the audience can feel sympathy.

Ashton's Alain shows yet another aspect of the sad clown or 'little man' and can, when subtly played, gain much sympathy because, while things seem to go right, he is so pleased with life. His delight first makes itself evident during his solo for Lise even though technical mistakes keep on happening. When he pulls himself up or corrects his placing or step he beams on the audience as, for example, when he finishes with his back after a *pirouette* and hastily turns to face them. The same happens during the *pas de deux* that is supposed to be with Lise. Each time they arrive at a pose, Colas somehow steals the expected kiss or holds Lise in the proper climax as Alain strikes what he believes to be the proper pose. He is always part of the total picture but facing the wrong way. Such a dance requires exact timing from all concerned, just as certain movements do in MacMillan's *Elite Syncopations* when the tall girl and the short boy dance to 'Alaskan Rag' or when the giggly couple dance in 'The Golden Hours'.

The above examples are all slightly parodied versions of classical dance steps. It is useful to point out that when using such materials choreographers must know their vocabulary very thoroughly and select movements through which they can emphasise the moment when disaster strikes. Such a moment arises when the short boy endeavours to catch the tall girl round the waist as she extends her leg to turn *à la seconde* but grabs her knee instead and has to creep round underneath. Some may complain that such tricks are too obvious. This is not so. The dance has to be so arranged that the mistake must appear accidental. Both Ashton and MacMillan take the technical aspects of their choreography very seriously. They know that just one small slip can make a joke in dance. Moreover, the dancers involved have to take this type of performance very seriously, even though they must be able to 'toss off' the mistakes with an air of surprised innocence.

Characters in National ballet

The above approach towards any type of character role is a very typically English trait and has been used in music halls, pantomimes and comedies for many years. It is this particular way of playing which makes Ashton's *La Fille Mal Gardée* what can be called a National Ballet in the same sense that both *The Firebird* and *Petrushka* can be called Russian National Ballets and *Rodeo* and *Fall River Legend* American. When choreographers wish to be patriotic by displaying the national origins of a company, school or ballet, they must not only be thoroughly conversant with that country's uniquely traditional folk arts but also be very sensitive to the way that native performers play in the popular theatre. It is not enough to give folk dances theatrical form by opening out their patterns, paying increased attention to the relationship of step to music and developing any unique style of movement. All these should also happen in character dance (see page 120). The collective behaviour of all the inhabitants as well as certain idiosyncrasies and possibly even eccentricities can make some contribution to the overall design. They can also emphasise features which belong exclusively to that one country.

Massine's *The Three-Cornered Hat* is possibly still the most important national ballet of Spain yet to be produced. Its story, music, décor and costumes were created by the Spaniards Alarcón, De Falla and Picasso. Yet the choreography is by a Russian who studied among the Spanish peasants and worked out his design with the help of a

Cinderella Ashton and English pantomime traditions
Shoe fitting (David Bintley, Deryck Rencher, Jonathan Cope)

particular peasant, a natural dancer, whose passion for dance was such that his life ended tragically when he found he was not to perform in the ballet. Such was his influence and so intense Massine's study and application of the knowledge gained that other versions of Spanish dance by native choreographers made no such impact. The great dancer Antonio was unable to match Massine's design even though each member of Antonio's company danced as to the manner born. Antonio was a star dancer and he could not take an objective view of the whole. His design focused on his brilliant performance of the various solos but otherwise filled the stage with authentic steps which played little part in making the action unfold.

Means of expression

While choreographers who wish to create a character and/or national ballet have an immense amount of material upon which to work, they must be very selective if they are to communicate the characteristic and/or purely nationalistic elements which will make a ballet unique. Moreover, as has been noted earlier, all character dance movements must be more strongly marked both physically and musically than the *demi-caractère* versions of the same steps. Similarly, all the poses and/or gestures performed by each character must be distinctly national, no matter how minor a part is being played.

127

The truly heroic character of Lemminkainen in the great Finnish epic *Kalevala* acts, according to the story, very much in the same way as the heroes of the Anglo-Saxon *Beowulf* or the French *Song of Roland* and many other heroic poems. Nevertheless he is uniquely different because he is not only a hero but also a powerful magician in the tradition of many Slav and Asiatic epics. In some ways, too, he behaves as the type of classical hero who ultimately became the *danseur noble* of classical ballet, because he always behaves nobly and truly. If the choreographer thinks he can use the purely classical vocabulary as the basis of his design it will fail to convey the totally different world from which this ancient epic emerged. It will not reflect the beliefs, behaviour, problems, wars and evil forces which give such colour and life to the narrative. Lemminkainen was able to weave and cast spells to win his way through to the end of his journey. He is a barbarian in the same way as the Polovtsian dancers in *Prince Igor*. If he were to conform to the strict rules of etiquette and combat guiding the *danseurs nobles* of the French opera-ballets, he would not demean himself by seizing the nearest thing at hand, the rudder from his boat, to put his adversary to flight. David Bintley's *The Swan of Tuonela* was one of the first attempts to create a ballet from the Finnish epic with music by Sibelius, a truly national composer from Finland. It successfully conveys something of this many faceted tale of daring behaviour.

To produce any kind of character and/or national ballet the choreographer should call on the three kinds of mime mentioned earlier, viz. conventional and occupational gesture and natural emotional expression.

Conventional gestures are valuable not only because they often appear in the epics themselves, but also because they are universally recognised as a means of communication in real life and have been used on the stage since the earliest days of the theatre. They must be performed and co-ordinated with the dance style and musical rhythms appropriate to the location where the story is being enacted.

They must also be performed and co-ordinated with the occupational gestures that belong to the location and that are employed by the particular inhabitants whose story, with its moods, emotions and actions, is being told.

This means that natural emotional expression must also be folded into the design. This is probably the most difficult material to handle because the many characters and nationalities involved in the various available libretti must express themselves as distinctively as they do in real life and the choreographer must try and ensure his design has some semblance of reality if it is to communicate meaning. It was in this particular field of difficulty that Balanchine sometimes showed his deep understanding. In his abstract ballets or interpretations of music, he rarely worried about the mood or emotional content of the music. Yet in *The Four Temperaments* he revealed very clearly and subtly how four very different types of person react to the mood suggested by Hindemith's music, whilst using his particular style of classical dance (see page 54).

If the choreographer is attempting to draw and communicate a moving picture of the individual character and physical attributes which permanently affect the manner of acting, feeling and thinking of their hero, heroine and entire cast, then they must study not only the general outline and background of their chosen story or theme, but also the beliefs, ways of life and traditions which have given life to the people and tales of different countries.

Modern style

There is a necessary distinction to be made between modern style and modern ballet.

In the modern style used by choreographers, they are to an increasing extent trying to do away with all the conventions inherent in the traditional techniques of classical and other styles. This has certainly led to a freeing of the body to give it a greater range of movement. The various schools of modern dance do, however, usually insist on a proper discipline and technique of movement. Without turn-out, tutus and *pointe* shoes the dancers' bodies still have the same physical apparatus as before and if bodies are to dance at all they must submit to some form of discipline. Even primitive tribes when dancing submit to the discipline imposed by their leaders. It is worth noting that such important modern choreographers as Kurt Jooss and Martha Graham and the leader of the Dance Theatre of Harlem, George Mitchell, insisted that their dancers have knowledge of some school of classical technique, to which they added other exercises to develop the flexibility of their dancers' bodies, athletic qualities and an ability to explore more thoroughly the space around them in all its dimensions.

The additional exercises certainly led to a greater use of patterns made by the dancers rolling or posturing over and on the floor. This gave greater depth to most of the patterns, but often made the dancers appear earthbound. It also led to closer contacts between the dancers as they moved from picture to picture within the design. From time to time this can be very beautiful but because there is a lack of continuity in the dance movement from one picture to the next, the resultant work often appears static. Alternatively, it may appear too acrobatic or athletic because the choreographer has been so concerned with the turning of the pages of a picture book that there is no explanation why one picture follows another and leads to another and yet another until the curtain falls.

Modern ballet

If the choreographer has 'subordinated tradition to harmonise with modern thought or modern terms of expression' (see page 12) then in a literal sense, the ballet is modern.

Since the publishers of Radcliffe Hall's *The Well of Loneliness* and Lawrence's *Lady Chatterley's Lover* were charged before the courts for contravening the laws of obscenity and both cases were lost by the Crown, any subject can be discussed in public. Novels, plays, films and documentaries, both serious and frivolous, have presented taboo subjects in English ballet. MacMillan's *The Invitation* was only one to have been staged by the Royal Ballet companies. A brief list shows how much ground he has covered since the strict rules of British censorship have been lifted.

rape and frustration	*The Invitation; Las Hermanas*
decadence and schizophrenia	*Mayerling; Manon*
madness	*The Playground*
incest	*My Brothers, My Sisters*
'Man's inhumanity to Man'	*The Burrow; A Distant Drummer*

It is important to note that these ballets were created by MacMillan whose aim has been to convince audiences that dance in ballet belongs to the reality of life and to show how life can be manipulated. He first described this in *Noctambules* which showed how the characters portrayed were manipulated by the Hypnotist. Manipulation was shown more dramatically in *A Distant Drummer*. The enormities of the Hitler regime and the Holocaust opened up many fields of research into the workings of minds not only of fanatics but also of the mentally disoriented or diseased. Such influences seriously affect all movement and behaviour, most noticeably in the works listed against 'Man's inhumanity to Man', where the 'little man' is manipulated by others.

To communicate the meaning of any story or theme based on real life, choreographers must take into account all the facets of modern thought and behaviour. They must then develop a style of movement which will convey the life of all their characters no matter how minor their roles in the unfolding of the action or theme. In other words, they must develop a style which will reveal not only the physical attributes of the characters but also their mental attitudes. Thus the choreographic design will describe not only personal moods, emotions and actions but also their effect on inter-personal relationships. It is the conflict between the players in any drama which heightens or when necessary relaxes the tension necessary for a climax to the plot.

However hard one may try to place a new ballet in any of the style categories already mentioned, it is noticeable that the basic style of dance used in any ballet is usually merged with another. This is because the choreographer has amalgamated the steps, poses and gestures to make a particular statement about the story, theme or music inspiring the work. For example: *Enigma Variations* could be called a character ballet because it describes 'the persons empictured within' by Elgar himself. Yet Ashton found ways of so moulding classical dance that the ladies even danced *sur les pointes* in so Edwardian a setting. The ballet could have been entered under the title of *demi-caractère*, but those people were not figments of the imagination. They really lived, were visualised by the composer, then the choreographer and recognised by old friends in the audience. Robbins' *Dances at a Gathering* could be called a romantic ballet because it uses classical technique coloured by natural emotional expression. It communicates the moods, sentiments and behaviour of young people meeting to enjoy each other's company as young people always do though not usually to Chopin's romantic music. In essence their behaviour is little different from that in *Fancy Free*. Yet this work was absolutely contemporary when produced. The three boys come directly from a battleship when they pick up three girls from the street. The dancing reflects the wartime atmosphere when shore leave was a cherished moment. Even though the boys and girls are figments of Robbins' imagination, their brief encounter is based in reality even to the introduction of popular dance steps and stylistic elements current during the 1939–45 war.

Both the above-mentioned works show that ballets based on the life of real people require that choreographers closely observe the characteristics and idiosyncrasies of all types of person and that they make them recognisable in order that they convey meaning. Yet the above ballets are different again from de Valois' *The Rake's Progress*, which was based on the reality of Hogarth's pictures. When these pictures were issued they were indeed contemporary because they were based on the evils of the day.

Today's audiences find them old-fashioned: yet many modern ballets deal with similar evils such as present-day problems with drugs, AIDS, mental handicap, racism, imprisonment and so on, in which the balletic interpretation makes the same impression if the choreographer has really studied the themes outlined in his subject.

These choreographers must create movements which display each protagonist's particular behaviour and reactions. Too often their movements are insufficiently defined because too much effort is made to shock, unlike the tightly controlled movements of characters in *The Rake's Progress* and *A Distant Drummer*.

In each of the three ballets discussed movements are not merely coloured by natural emotional expression but often by conventional and occupational gesture, which appear to spring from each dancer's physical and mental reactions to each situation as it arises.

A comparison of such different ballets as *Enigma Variations*, *Fancy Free* and *The Rake's Progress* emphasises how important it is for young choreographers to remember that ballet is an art of the general as well as of the particular. This arises from the fact that no one really dances through life, though doing so once the curtain has risen. *Enigma Variations* is a unique ballet about particular people at a particular time and in a particular environment – the characters were even recognised by old friends (see page 53). Yet *Mayerling*, although based on what little facts are known of the life of Rudolf of Austria, barely suggests reality. In an attempt to show the decadence and revolutionary ideas endemic in the court life of the Emperor Francis Joseph, MacMillan overloaded his plot with incident. He thus turned what could have been a tragedy into a melodrama, i.e. 'a sensational dramatic piece with crude appeals to the emotions' (O.E.D.). Even so, it was the first successful attempt in this genre because it gave its performers an opportunity to reveal their talents as actor-dancers. Although they were playing stereotyped conspirators, innocents, prostitutes, courtiers and lackeys each role had a personality of its own and thus a semblance of reality. This had not happened on such a scale before and encouraged MacMillan to stage another biographical work, *Isadora*, which followed the pattern of his earlier *Anastasia*. Neither was very successful because the characters were not fully defined and the plots were confused by too much use of stage effects. MacMillan's *The Burrow*, based on the real diary of Anne Frank, was possibly the most explicit and moving of all his efforts to depict reality in terms of dance (see page 30).

The classification of today's ballets becomes more difficult as their stories, themes and music get more complicated. Very occasionally, the opposite happens, e.g. in Robbins' *Glass Pieces* to John Cage's 'minimal music', the constant repetition of musical phrases paralleled by dance phrases lost the interest of an audience bored with too much meaningless to-ing and fro-ing.

Modern style

After studying the above ballets it may well be asked what is modern style? Before attempting a new definition (see page 12) it would be better to consider two important factors, namely the art of the general and the art of the particular.

The art of the general

General 'completely or almost universal including or affecting nearly all parts' (O.E.D.)

The art of the general in dance means that the choreographer must understand the working of a dancer's body and its ability to respond physically to any demand for movement. Dance technique is more embracing than that for any other physical activity such as sports, gymnastics, athletics and so on. As explained elsewhere classical technique is the most demanding. It has evolved from the simplest folk through the mannered court and finally to the expert classical dance. It is designed to display both dancer and dance to the best advantage from the audience's point of view. It is a strict discipline upon which to build. Its exponents are trained to feel how to move with each part of their bodies and to know how their movements must be co-ordinated to produce one or another step or pose. Each movement is complete in itself but must flow into the next and become part of the total choreographic design. Correctly practised such movements ensure that each dancer can perform in many different ways the four vital movements of which the body is capable (the legs may be turned in or out), viz. to bend, stretch, rise and rotate. These active steps (or verbs) can also be interpreted as meaning to relax, contract, raise, lift or jump, turn or twist (see pages 50 and 69). The muscles must be trained to counter-balance each other appropriately if the dancer is to defy the laws of gravity whatever the style of dance. Even if it seems inappropriately mentioned, any fall used as part of the design has to be carefully worked out. Every movement on stage has to be a conscious effort on the dancer's part if it is to make its proper impact.

When performing any movement in the classical vocabulary dancers are drawing straight, angled or rounded lines which affect one or all parts of the body. They can fill the space in which they move by the amalgamation of steps, poses and gestures, which can travel in any direction and dimension (see page 69). The *enchaînements* can be danced to any time signature, phrasing or tempo. Although some modern dancers do without music in the accepted sense of that term, they rarely do without rhythmic phrasing. If they do they have forgotten that, like them, every member of their audience 'has an inborn sense of measuring time... Without a sense of rhythm, our sense of time is devoid of landmarks' and, as Frank Howes added later, 'and sense' (see page 68).

The art of the particular

Particular 'the relation to one as distinguished from another' (O.E.D.)

The question now to be asked is where does the art of the particular begin in the creation of style? It has already been noted that the movements in Ashton's five abstract ballets have been coloured by the music, its period and sometimes by the composer's own thoughts (see page 42). Each of those ballets can also be said to have dimension and linear patterns which can be roughly described as follows:

Symphonic Variations Lines are widely structured, flowing and straight rather than rounded, with no hard edges.

Scènes de Ballet The lines are straighter and more angled than usual in classical dance. They are precise in detail yet from time to time break away from the formal patterns of Petipa's well-ordered conventions.

Birthday Offering Precise and accurately placed *enchaînements* and *épaulement* give a clear definition to each step and pose as it takes its place in a perfectly balanced design.

Rhapsodie The patterns fill the stage in all its dimensions whilst remaining within the more conventional patterns of older ballets. Because the patterns are forever changing shape, the lines are more lightly etched and give greater fluidity and excitement to the dance.

Similar remarks could be made about the abstract ballets by Balanchine, MacMillan and others. Since choreographers discarded the conventions which kept 'ballet dancing' in a straightjacket (after Fokine taught that it was 'the whole body that dances', not merely the legs), the classical vocabulary has provided ideal material on which to build for those who understand its technique.

It was and still is the extraordinary pictorial value of the linear patterns and forms created by Nijinska for *Les Noces* which emphasises more clearly than any other ballet the need for every choreographer to keep strict control over the mass of material needed to make a single work. At the time of its production, Diaghilev was convinced that another truly Russian ballet was needed, traditional in essence but reflecting the revolutionary ideas of contemporary artists working in Russia as well as Paris.

Stravinsky had started composing *Les Noces* before 1913 and often played it to Diaghilev, gradually simplifying his ideas until it became the present cantata for voices, four pianos and percussion. Similarly the artist Goncharova's original gorgeously coloured designs for traditional Russian wedding costumes were made austere in keeping with Nijinska's demands for simplicity even though *Les Noces* was to be danced *sur les pointes*. She felt that their use 'would elongate the dancers' silhouettes and thus resemble the figures of Byzantine Saints'. Anyone acquainted with ancient ikons will recognise how acutely she has captured their essence. The ballet is also based on the traditional Russian wedding rites which prepare both Bride and Groom for the ceremony before the wedding feast. Yet *Les Noces* was also of its own time, 1923. It was strongly influenced by the contemporary art movement known as Constructivism, which was being energetically pursued. It has been defined as: 'The minimal requirements needed to fill a picture surface meaningfully, whilst combining various materials into forms that usually do not depict anything' (O.E.D.).

The forms depicted by Nijinska are far from meaningless. Not only do they reflect the significance of each part of the ancient ritual, but also the solemn chant of the singers during the ceremonies and later the raucous shouts of the guests at the feast. She displays how to build living structures of pictorial importance by weaving individual dancers or groups deliberately and solemnly so that they frequently pause in a meaningful picture of distinctive shape. These are the full stops to a paragraph that give the audience an opportunity to sum up – as it were – how the Bride's hair is cut; why the men convey the Groom to the Bride's house; how the Bride and Groom are blessed by their parents; and so on. By so phrasing each paragraph and bringing each incident to a proper conclusion, Nijinska gives both dancers and audience time to consider what has been done and what is yet to happen.

The nature of the formal shapes made by the dancers' bodies and limbs as they move into and hold a picture must be evaluated. Nijinska insisted on the use of the *pointes* in order to emphasise the elongated portraits of the Byzantine Saints, thus the dancers' bodies mostly face the audience but their arms and legs turn inwards and are seen mostly in profile. The angles made at the elbows, shoulders, knees and ankle joints are clearly visible. Those of the arms are particularly interesting because the fists are either clenched or the fingers flattened thus the lines and shapes made only appear slightly rounded by the folds in the sleeves. The dancers drawing these straight, angled and very slightly rounded lines have to work accurately and be correctly aligned with their neighbours in each temporary grouping. Each grouping has to be correctly aligned with the other whether it precedes, balances or follows another. Yet each must be within the whole framework. This is particularly so in the last dance, when the

Bride and Groom are watched by all as they solemnly walk together through the doorway into their room. This moment is the proper conclusion that sums up what has now been accomplished. Few, if any other choreographers, have consistently controlled the very personal and strongly motivated style for a single ballet. It is starkly simple and exactly states its purpose demonstrating that even the most primitive of beliefs and traditional practices are valid materials on which to build not only the style but the dramatic content of a ballet. It emphasises, too, man's primitive belief that if his real life task is to be successful, then it must first be enacted in the magic made by dance (see page 15).

Les Noces practises the art of the general and the art of the particular at one and the same time. This should be the important factor of every ballet. Nijinska's design reveals the group personality of peasants attending a traditional Russian wedding. They already know the part they have to play to ensure its success. Not even the Bride and Groom stand out. They are dressed like everyone else. In fact they scarcely dance at all. Yet because of their passive acceptance of the ministrations of their neighbours they become the focus of attention. The group activities ensure that each phase of the ceremony is performed according to tradition. The design emphasises the importance of creating a style which will define not only the time, place and action, but also the characters portrayed. The technical or general style creates the structure and atmosphere of the whole. In other words, the particular becomes the general.

A similar analysis could be made of MacMillan's *Requiem*. The general structure is drawn from specific rules of movement. It comprises elements from both modern and

Requiem   MacMillan's modern classicism and use of Blake's drawings: the Mourners (The Royal Ballet led by Bryony Brind) . . .

. . . *Pie Jesu* (Lesley Collier)

classical techniques ensuring that the lines and patterns made by the dancers' bodies are more expressively stretched and angled and less rounded than usual, because so much is danced with tense emotion. These shapes are built into moving pictures which are inspired by those drawn by Blake to illustrate stories from the Bible. Because the dancers' gestures register despair, anger, appeals for help and then resignation, the emotional content of the whole is overwhelming. No one stands out, although some emerge from the group in brief solos to express their personal sense of loss. But these soloists are the links between one group or grouping and another. Everyone is part of the whole design. Yet when the stage is empty of mourners, there emerges a solitary dancer and the entire mood changes. She is a child-like figure who dances innocently to Fauré's *Pie Jesu*. As she explores the vast cathedral-like space with her movements, she marvels at the shapes and lines every part of her body can make to fill the space. She is supremely happy merely to dance in such a setting and to such music. She represents hope and it is the purity of MacMillan's design which shows how 'the whole body dances'. When the mourners return, all passion spent, recognising the eventuality of death and now resigned to their loss, the child-like figure can be raised on high in the final Amen (see page 46).

Technical characteristics

It is the very particular choreographic style that MacMillan created for the child-like figure in *Requiem* that emphasises more strongly than any other of today's ballets the need for choreographers to explore dance itself. Only when they have examined what hands, arms, legs and feet, body and above all the head can do in isolation and then in harmony with the story, theme or music, can they set out and create a style which will be general in structure and particular in texture, with the right quality, mood, emotion, action and character. The structure will determine the lines and shapes needed to fill the dimensions and, when needed, help to create the atmosphere and mood of the whole. Choreographers must then decide how many and which details they need to add to disclose the particular features of the story, theme and/or music that they wish to communicate.

The exploration of what each part of the body can express in isolation and then in co-ordination with the rest is possibly the most important aspect of a choreographer's work if it seeks to be modern in spirit and technique. Different fields of research have disclosed the many different factors that can affect both physical and mental behaviour. All such studies have influenced every form of art in some way. Dance seems to have been affected most by psychological studies initiated by Freud and others and first exploited by Rudolf von Laban and Mary Wigman. Such theories have helped to free dancers from the strict conventions of classical technique and to develop what can be called body language. Such theories also opened up other fields in which to search for inspiration. The danger is that too much reliance can be placed on intellectual exercises with resulting works only comprehensible to those studying the same theories. Nevertheless it is worth citing some instances where the continual use of one or a very few gestures can fully describe the feelings of some characters and convey their reactions to the circumstances of the plot or theme.

Hands Ashton described the innocence, piety and wonder of the Bride at the event to be when he created the exquisitely detailed hand movements in *The Wise Virgins*, as he did for *La Péri* and *Madame Chrysanthème*. Also there was his own final gesture of hopelessness in *Nocturne* (see page 109).

MacMillan created a strange gesture for Rudolf in *Mayerling*; he frequently clasps his hand against the side of his head and ear as if to ease the pain of his deteriorating brain in order to shut out the rumours surrounding his every activity. This gesture becomes more strongly evident and unpredictable as more and more events crowd in until both hands are used to shut out thoughts of the suicide he feels is inevitable.

Legs In Ashton's *The Two Pigeons* and *A Month in the Country* there is the ecstatic quiver of the leg which continues upwards through the body until the Young Girl or Natalia and Vera can rest their head on their lover's shoulder as they embrace. The ecstasy of love being felt to rise through the body 'from the tips of the toes, to the tips of the fingers and from the heart to the head' was said by Anna Pavlova to be the essence of dance. And it is in so many of Ashton's *pas de deux* where the truth of those words is always evident. There is a particularly fine example in the last *pas de deux* of *La Fille Mal Gardée* where Lise and Colas weave themselves into an embrace which is so tender, gentle and loving that it arrives at the end of a phrase as the most natural thing in the world.

There are other delicious gestures drawing attention to the feet in *La Fille Mal Gardée* such as Mother Simone gently tapping her clogs as if thanking them for

Mayerling   MacMillan's use of specific gesture
Mary Vetsera gives her willing body to the tormented Rudolf (Fiona Chadwick, Wayne Eagling)

allowing her to show off her particular style of dance. It emphasises that she is not the awful old termagant she has so far seemed to be. A similar tiny gesture takes on the same value when Alain rubs one foot up and down the other leg when the girls tickle him. This not only allows him to indulge in more of those awkward movements, which make his first solo such a wonderful parody of classical dance, but shows him as the pathetic clown, always the butt of everyone's laughter.

Heads However some of the most expressive movements are made by the head because the way in which it is used can draw attention to the look on the face. As John Weaver said (1708): 'The face is the mirror of the soul', and in dance 'must speak through the eyes'. The mere fact of lowering the head in suffering and despair or raising it in anger or appeals for help as the dancers do in MacMillan's *Requiem* vividly conveys the tragedy and sorrow that has befallen these mourners. Yet it is the head movements of the young girl as she dances to *Pie Jesu* that are so telling. She actively watches the lines made by her arms and legs as they form varying shapes. She marvels that they flow so easily to fill the vast space in which she moves. She raises her eyes to the wonder of its beauty, sometimes tilting her head as if listening to the music echoing round her. In *Gloria* every movement seems tense even when characters are looking tenderly at those they love for they are always aware of the next leave-taking. This is particularly poignant towards the end when both girls and boys, the youth of their generation, disappear forever in the tragedy of war

Choreographers today choose to interpret a vast range of subjects through what can be termed the purely physical movements of the body, sometimes coloured by moods ranging from the tragic to the comic and even the ridiculous. They sometimes create what can be called highly intellectual concepts such as the case-history of a mental patient, which require a distinctive style. Unfortunately these histories are not always clear owing to the limitations of the human body and its inability verbally to state the problems. Dance is a language of silence. Everything has to be expressed by movement alone, coloured by expression. It is impossible exactly to define what is modern dance because the body is the same that has danced for hundreds of years. Choreographers cannot in any way change the ways in which their dancers move. The audience recognise physical movement for itself alone whereas those who theorise and attempt to define what they mean by such terms as post or neo-modern, contemporary, avant-garde, etc. base their works on intellectual concepts which need to be discussed in words. Thus the audience fail to understand everything that is offered. Dance is firstly a physical activity and if it is obscured by complicated costumes, props, machinery, lighting and stage effects, it ceases to be relevant to anything but the cleverness of the producer.

In a letter Ashton once answered such bewilderment by quoting:
'If we shadows have offended
Think but this and all is mended
That you have but slumbered here
Whilst we shadows did appear.'

(Photo of Anthony Dowell)

Index of ballets

Names of choreographers, followed by names of composers, are given in brackets
after titles of ballets.
Numbers in italics refer to illustrations

General index

Numbers in italics refer to illustrations